JAMES P. RAFFINI
received his Doctorate of Educational Psychology
from Northern Illinois University
and is Professor of Education
at the University of Wisconsin-Whitewater.

A SPECTRUM BOOK

PRENTICE-HALL, INC., Englewood Cliffs, N.J. 07632

James P. Raffini

DISCIPLINE
negotiating conflicts
with today's kids

Library of Congress Cataloging in Publication Data

RAFFINI, JAMES P
  Discipline, negotiating conflicts wtih today's kids.

  (A Spectrum Book)
  Bibliography: p.
  Includes index.
    1. School discipline.   2. Teacher-student relation-
ships.   3. Problem children—Education.   I. Title.
LB3012.R33   371.5   80-14626
ISBN 0-13-215731-4
ISBN 0-13-215723-2 (pbk.)

Editorial/production supervision and interior design by Carol Smith
Cover design by Honi Werner
Manufacturing buyer: Cathie Lenard

10 9 8 7 6 5 4 3 2 1

Printed in the United States of America

PRENTICE-HALL INTERNATIONAL, INC., *London*
PRENTICE-HALL OF AUSTRALIA PTY., LIMITED, *Sydney*
PRENTICE-HALL OF CANADA, LTD., *Toronto*
PRENTICE-HALL OF INDIA PRIVATE LIMITED, *New Delhi*
PRENTICE-HALL OF JAPAN, INC., *Tokyo*
PRENTICE-HALL OF SOUTHEAST ASIA PTE. LTD., *Singapore*
WHITEHALL BOOKS LIMITED, *Wellington, New Zealand*

*To fair winds
and following seas for all,
but especially
for my stouthearted shipmates—
Carol, Leslie, and Eric*

CONTENTS

3

PREVENTING DISRUPTIVE BEHAVIOR

*(a gram of prevention
is worth a kilogram of cure)* 52

4

TEACHER-STUDENT DIALOGUE

(it's like talking to a brick wall!) 76

5

DEALING WITH
DISRUPTIVE BEHAVIOR

(how can I fix their wagons?) 100

Teachers and parents agree: "Lack of discipline" is the number-one concern in American education. Unfortunately, the questions as to what we mean by "discipline" and how to get more of it produce more disagreement than a bowl of bean and garlic soup. This book is based on the assumption that a traditional approach to discipline, based on irrational obedience to authority and enforced by rewards and punishments, is no longer functional in today's society. Many children are beginning to demand a literal interpretation of the concept of American Democracy. Granted, "kiddie lib" is a difficult pill to swallow. It produces resentment and confusion in the minds

PREFACE

of many teachers and parents. Smiling a lot and letting kids do as they please is not the answer. Doormats and dictators are both destined to doom in today's schools and homes.

Various chapters in this book present other, different solutions to the problems of disruptiveness. Many of the things we do as teachers and parents *cause* the disruptive behavior we hope to avoid. Chapter 2 discusses types of and reasons for disruptiveness, and Chapter 3 examines ways to *prevent* the occurrence of disruptions caused by teachers, parents, and the curriculum. On the other hand, some children are willing to destroy the school and home environments in attempts to satisfy their personal needs. Chapter 4 presents a way to improve communication with disruptive kids regardless of the cause. A method for dealing with disruptions caused by students trying to meet their needs at the expense of others is presented in Chapter 5. The method, called *behavior negotiating*, is based on a synthesis of the approaches advocated by William Glasser, Thomas Gordon, and Rudolf Dreikurs. Problems with using humanistic methods in inner city classrooms are also discussed in the chapter, along with a section that offers specific recommendations to parents.

The ideas contained in this book are the result of my public school teaching experiences, working with many teachers in inservice workshops and graduate courses, my experience as a parent, and ten years of reading about the problem of school discipline. I have attempted to give credit to those ideas taken from other writers. It has been difficult during the past years to determine where my ideas begin and others leave off. I apologize if I have not always kept this distinction clear.

I am grateful to Mr. Keith Collins and the Janesville School Board for enabling me to return to the public school classroom after ten years of university teaching, and to the administrators and staff at Edison Junior High School for making me feel welcome. I offer special thanks to my friends and colleagues: to Lee Rexroat for being a good listener; to Ron Hering, Ike Schaffer, Robin Schwaba, Mert

Manley, and Bob Schissel for their encouragement; and to Barb Herlihy, Chuck Park, and Jon Carlson for their valuable suggestions and comments when reviewing the manuscript. Finally, I would like to thank the many teachers who, as graduate students in my classes, shared their classroom problems and worked together to examine alternatives. This book is truly the product of those encounters.

Students, Don't Push Your Teacher Down the Stairs on Friday

Who Will Listen?

Don't Smile Until Christmas

Nobody Can Teach Anyone Anything

Help! These Kids Are Driving Me Crazy

To Hell With Kids

These desperate cries for help and words of advice are actually titles of books—books designed to help teachers and parents replenish their depleting arsenal of ways for dealing with discipline problems. The goal of this book is similar; its approach, however, is both optimistic and humanistic. Although I'm a psychologist, I've

1

INTRODUCTION

(what these kids need is...)

tried not to make this a psychology book. A friend once said, "The best thing to do with a psychology book is to use it to spank children."

Having been tagged a "discipline problem" myself, I have always been intrigued by that label. During those twelve years of apprenticeship required to receive a high school diploma, I was continually getting into and out of "trouble." I don't think I did anything terribly bad, but somehow I found myself spending many long hours in that lonesome desk located in front of the room, in the hallway, or in the cloakroom. While attending a parochial grade school, I also spent a great deal of time on my knees praying for forgiveness. Now, many years later, I find remembering the details of my disruptive behavior difficult, but some of the images and feelings remain.

I believe I was in the fifth grade when I arrived at the conclusion that most nuns hated me. I had always been somewhat fearful of them as they towered over me in their black and white habits, with only a round face and eyes of granite showing through. I guess I felt a little cheated and envious knowing that they were guaranteed a place in heaven, while I was assured of spending an eternity of shoveling coal.

Fortunately, I found consolation in knowing that my best friend, Eugene, would be with me down there. He and I lived in the same neighborhood; and since he was also certain that the nuns hated him, we became close friends. We would often try to guess how many days were in an eternity as we walked home from school each day looking for pop bottles and cigarette butts. We never could understand why souls destined to live in the fires of hell wouldn't burn. It seemed like we talked for hours about what type of guy the devil really was or if the nuns actually shaved their heads. Occasionally, we would even share our impure thoughts during those long walks.

I never blamed the nuns for hating us. After all, neither of us was a good student, and we did talk a lot when we weren't supposed to. Our fifth-grade nun was bothered most by the little signal Eugene and I used when we wanted to get each other's attention. We would place our tongues on the roofs of our mouths and then push up and back. The suction would make a clicking noise that could be varied in intensity and tone by simply moving our cheeks. We both became quite skilled at this and practiced each day on the way home. By the time we had finished sixth grade, we could carry on a complete conversation with nothing more than the "click," as we called it.

I never sat next to Eugene at school; the seating chart was always designed so that he would be at one end of the room while I was at the other. Consequently, the temptation to use the "click" was always great, especially during language arts time. That was when we spent hours developing the fine art of diagramming sentences. Neither of us was very good at it. I didn't mind drawing the lines; they were fun to make. My problem was I never could decide where all the words were supposed to go. At first I tried to get them right. They reminded me of putting puzzles together (something I was very good at); but after nouns, verbs, and adjectives, I became totally confused. (This last sentence would really be a challenge!) Anyway, after trying for a few minutes, one of us would give up and begin to use the "click." The other would then check out the nun to see if she had heard it. If she hadn't, he would then start giggling and return the click. This would continue back and forth until we were inevitably caught. One of us was either reprimanded or moved to the lonesome desk, depending upon the mood of the nun, which I believe was directly related to whether we had a Low or High Mass before school. (We were all required to attend unless you could make yourself look sick.) There appeared to be no pattern as to which of us would have to suffer, but I do remember complaining to

Eugene that it was unfair that I had to log more time in the cloak-room than he.

Our sixth-grade nun finally ended our "games." She was an older, husky woman who had the ability to make all in the room tremble with terror when she spoke. Eugene and I came to the agreement that the sole purpose for her existence was to make one or both of us cry. At some point during the year she had been able to elicit tears from each of our other friends who transgressed her rigid order. By spring, we were the last holdouts. We had spent a great deal of time analyzing her various methods and techniques, and we had developed a pact never to give in.

I expect I shall never forget that fateful day when she got me. I was standing in line to go to recess (we *always* stood in lines). Unthinkingly, I committed the second mortal sin of her class: "talk-ing to my neighbor." (The first was getting out of line.) Having had a Requiem High Mass that morning, I knew I was in trouble. She pulled me aside by the arm and instructed the others to go outside. Seconds later, I found myself backed against the wall with her hand on my chin forcing me to look up at her red and angry face (she knew Eugene and I always looked at our feet in times like this). I don't remember the words she used or even her tone of voice; but as I stared into her wrathful eyes, an uncontrollable urge overwhelmed my entire body. Try as I did, I could not stop the tear that formed. As it slowly rolled down my cheek, her hand let loose my chin. I somehow managed to avoid looking at Eugene the rest of the day, but he must have sensed what had happened, because he was also silent as we walked home that afternoon. . .

To be fair to the ladies in black and white, during seven years of parochial education I encountered many nuns who were warm and sensitive. Their caring made it possible for me to survive that envi-ronment. Nevertheless, a few left painful and indelible memories.

While many educators believe that discipline problems are most rampant during the junior high years, my own behavior seemed to improve. Eugene moved to a different part of town and continued in parochial schools, while I transferred to the public schools. The new environment, along with the discovery of girls, seemed to help keep me out of the principal's office.

High school, however, found me back to my old self. Achieving some success on the gridiron helped keep me out of serious trouble; but cutting classes, detentions, and staying after school for lectures on the merits of good behavior were all commonplace for me. I guess you might say I was just an all-around screw-off.

Since the thought of going to college never crossed my mind until late in my senior year, I was free of the burden of having to get ready for it. I was usually placed in the non-college-bound courses, and I did roughly average work. I remember little from those classes except that I disliked English (even though we were no longer required to diagram), that Social Studies were okay, that shop was fun, and that I actually enjoyed math.

Many of the teachers found this last point rather peculiar. I was genuinely excited about math and took every course available. As a result, I found myself sitting in Advanced Algebra and Trigonometry classes with all of the top-tracked, college-bound "good" guys. It seemed that you were either a good guy or a bad guy at our school; and although I was usually put in the latter category, some teachers became confused when I was caught helping some of the good guys with their math problems. (I even taught a few the subtle techniques of the underage procurement of a six-pack or bottle of Silver Satin.)

My life changed rapidly during my senior year. We had a successful football season, and athletic scholarships became readily available. This was all a bit confusing at first, since I had never considered college and was totally unfamiliar with the idea. I recall the shock and disappointment I felt walking around the campus of Notre Dame and discovering it was an all boys' school. I eventually accepted a scholarship to a Big Ten School that was known for its night life. After three semesters of frolicking in this new world, I flunked out. Evidently some of the faculty believed that attendance at class, grade point averages, and progress toward a degree were important. When I was informed by the registrar that my attendance was no longer desired, the football coach advised me that I could stay on if I would simply transfer to the College of Agriculture. Having spent two summers working in onion and potato fields, I was certain that this life was not for me. After leaving college and then working for a couple of months on building construction, I was convinced that a life of labor wasn't for me either, so I enrolled in a small state university. Recalling only an occasional discussion with the Dean of Students about appropriate residence hall behavior, I guess I was no longer considered a discipline problem.

When I graduated with a degree in Secondary Education, the boot was quickly placed on the other foot. Instead of causing discipline problems, I was now expected to stop them. Working as a Social Studies teacher, football and basketball coach, equipment manager, and part-time janitor in a rural high school of 180 students, I encountered few problems. Sure, an unwary student would occasionally step out of line, but a stern, icy look, coupled with a raise of the eyebrows would usually instill fear and compliance. When this tactic failed, a bark and a growl, followed by a one-way ticket to the principal's office, always brought the desired results. Leaving high school teaching for graduate work in Counseling and Educational Psychology continued to keep me oblivious to the ulcer-causing concern of today's educators. Not until I began teaching graduate courses in Educational Psychology did I become aware of the many teachers who were clamoring for ways to cope with the nitty-gritty problems faced hour by hour in their lonely, frustrating, and sometimes hostile classrooms.

In an attempt to help teachers explore these problems, I created a seminar entitled "Understanding and Dealing with Disruptive Classroom Behavior." The first objective was to develop an atmosphere that would allow teachers to examine their implicit assumptions regarding student behavior. How do we expect students to behave? What do they do that drives us up a wall? A second goal was to help teachers look at some of their own behavior, which might inadvertently be contributing to the difficulties they were facing. Few of us consciously set about to create our own discipline problems, but often our actions and reactions have their effects. "I know I'm not a good student, but when teachers yell at me and treat me like garbage, I try to treat them the same way." This comment was made by one of the "live ones" we would find on the streets and bring to class. Finally, through discussion and role playing, we examined some of the strategies for dealing with those students whose favorite indoor sport is hassling teachers.

I enjoyed teaching the course and learned a great deal about the frustrations of school teachers. Nevertheless, my own experience in dealing with discipline problems was still vicarious: I shared in the many difficulties these teachers, as my students, were facing, but their problems were not mine. I could offer suggestions and alternatives based on my reading and my own experience as a troublemaker; but when Mike, the curly-haired fifth-grader, decided to streak the noon hour playground, or when Tom, the angry and lonely high school junior, decided to take a poke at his math teacher, *I* didn't have to deal with them.

In an attempt to find out for myself if things were as bad as my teacher/students were implying, I decided to take a leave from the university to go back and teach in the public school classroom. Most professors of Education recognize the need and value of returning to the schools, but the details of such a move make the possibility remote. After persistently wading through mounds of red tape with the help of a colleague who was a school board member, I was fortunate in obtaining a half-time reassignment as a junior high school Social Studies teacher. Part of my salary was provided by the university and the remainder by the school system. Not only did this arrangement provide me with an opportunity to teach an eighth-grade Social Studies class and a ninth-grade Social Studies class, but it also allowed me a prep period to work with students individually. I would be in the building from noon until 4 PM each day. The school, located in the industrial area of a moderately sized Midwestern city, had an enrollment of 1,500 seventh-, eighth-, and ninth-grade students. It had developed a reputation for its discipline problems, but I later believed the reputation was undeserved, as the students appeared no different from those in other schools of comparable size and socio-economic level.

Assigned to the Social Studies "pod" (or classroom), I was to become part of a five-member team. Two of the team members had previously been students of mine at the university, but we agreed that I would be introduced as Mr. Raffini, a new student teacher. I appeared a bit old for that role, but the students seemed to accept it in spite of the gray hair. The classroom (or pod) was a huge non-walled area composed of five teaching stations. The building was designed around the concept of "open education," but one sliding door had been installed in the pod, and a requisition had been filed for another. The curriculum appeared to be well organized. The ninth-graders were to study units of Crime and Justice, Urban Problems, The Consumer, and Drugs. My eighth-graders would deal with topics in History, Anthropology, Geography, and Political Science. What I share in the remainder of this book has been both tempered and reinforced by this experience.

DISCIPLINE AS OBEDIENCE

While recent Gallup Polls of education rank "lack of discipline" as the number-one concern of both parents and educators, such a concern is not new.

Our youths love luxury. They have bad manners, contempt for authority; they show disrespect for their elders, and love to chatter in place of exercise. Children are now tyrants, not the servants of their households. They no longer rise when their elders enter the room. They contradict their parents, chatter before company, gobble up their food, and tyrannize their teachers. (Socrates, 400 BC)

This classic lament of Socrates concerning the youth of his day could easily be attributed to the local barber, druggist, filling station attendant, or college professor.

What appears to be new, however, is the frustration that teachers and parents face when attempting to make the traditional techniques of control work with today's kids. I believe that part of the frustration is a result of confusion surrounding the word "discipline." For many, the word is synonymous with obedience—"Do what I want you to do when I want you to do it." The backbone for this point of view has developed from the belief that it is important to teach students a strong, unquestioning regard for authority.

Whether or not you agree with this definition of discipline, to make it work, the authority must be able to establish at least one of the following three contingencies:

1. *He or she must be able to develop a strong feeling of* respect *from those being controlled.*

2. *If this is not possible, the authority must be able to develop a system of* rewards *or* reinforcements *that makes it beneficial for those being controlled to do what they are told.*

3. *If neither of these is effective, the authority must be able to instill in those being controlled a* fear *of the consequences for not doing what they are commanded to do.*

The apparent ineffectiveness of traditional approaches to discipline might well be traced to an erosion of these three contingencies.

First, unquestioned respect for the controlling authority (parent or teacher) seems to be undergoing a change. In the past, most teachers and parents could demand respect simply as a function of their role. Placed in a position of authority over others, a person was entitled to and could expect the respect of those being controlled. Today, this implicit respect appears to be changing. Many students no longer respect their teachers simply because of their position. Even being addressed as Mr., Mrs., Miss, Ms., or Dr. cannot assure the respect of the individual bearing the title. In many cases, the more insistent teachers become in demanding such respect, the more unlikely they are to receive it. Nevertheless, some teachers are still capable of receiving the heartfelt esteem and admiration of their students. These fortunate few have learned that respect can no longer be demanded—*it must be earned*. Failure to recognize this transition has contributed much to the frustration in today's homes and classrooms. The process of earning respect will be discussed later in this chapter and in Chapter 3.

The second contingency, a system of rewards or reinforcements, also appears to be in jeopardy. Traditionally, teachers have used verbal approval, privileges, gold stars, high grades, M&Ms, and hundreds of other goodies to reward students for obedience. Verbal approval, in the form of positive comments, praise, and encouragement, has always been among the strongest rewards or reinforcements available to teachers and parents. Unfortunately, with the erosion of respect, such verbal approval loses its effectiveness in influencing behavior. If my students see me as detached and aloof, and if I have not taken the time to earn their respect as a worthwhile and significant person, then my comments—like "Good work, Johnnie" and "Well done, Suzie"—fall on deaf ears. The use of tangible rewards like gold stars, candy bars, and privileges can still have some positive effect on students in the lower grades. However, many teachers in the junior and senior high schools are finding it more and more difficult to come up with reinforcements that have enough incentive to control the behavior of their recalcitrant students. The situation is further complicated when attention or approval from friends is more desired than that offered by the teacher. I have seen many situations when peer approval was awarded to behavior that was exactly the opposite of that demanded by the authority.

If we try to enforce a traditional view of discipline based on obedience, without internal respect for authority or without a system of strong incentives, then to make it work, we have no choice but to rely on the third contingency—fear. Fortunately or unfortunately, many teachers are finding it increasingly more difficult to scare kids. Many of the students we label as "discipline problems" are simply no longer afraid of authority. The teacher–student (T–S) scenario often goes like this:

T: *Johnnie, I've asked you a dozen times today to stop your fooling around and pay attention. If you interrupt one more time, I'm going to have to give you an F on this unit.*

S: *So, give me an F. This stuff is boring anyway.* [He knows he will probably still get a D in the course because he does do some work, and he's certain that the teacher doesn't want him back next year.]

T: *If you keep talking like that, young man, you're going to be finding yourself serving a detention!*

S: *I don't care, what's another detention? I already have 42 to serve; a few more won't make much difference.*

T: *We'll just see what your parents have to say about that, young man, when I call them this afternoon.*

S: *Go ahead, my ol' lady says she can't do anything with me either.*

T: *That does it! You can go down and talk to the vice-principal about your insolence.*

S: *Fine, anything to get the hell outta here. Besides, I've been down there all morning.*

Such threats of physical punishment, bad grades, detentions, or expulsions, which were somewhat effective in keeping kids in line in the past, have lost much of their effectiveness today. Sure, some teachers are still capable of instilling such fear, but they have to work harder at it. Some even appear to be born with this natural ability: My sixth-grade nun was one! I've also seen teachers who, on the surface, come on strong and appear to be tougher than nails. Deep down, however, they're really old softies with hearts of gold who love their kids, and, more importantly, the kids know it.

Blind Obedience

We must examine the whole idea surrounding the definition of discipline as unquestioned obedience. There's nothing innately wrong with obedience; we all know that chaos would result without it.

What's important is that we realize that blind obedience, for the sake of obedience, can be a very destructive force in society. Stanley Milgram has conducted some fantastic research on the subject, which has far-reaching implications.[1] He asked over a thousand people from all walks of life to participate in a research study of the effects of punishment on learning and memory. While he used several variations in his methodology, his general procedure was to take two individuals at a time, telling them that one was to be the "teacher" for the study and the other the "student." Unknown to the teacher, the individual assigned the role of "student" was a paid actor collaborating with Milgram. The actor/student was then wired with electrodes. The teacher, taken to a different room, was seated in front of an ominous electronic "shock generator" with a line of thirty switches ranging from "Slight Shock" to "Danger—Severe Shock." The teacher was instructed to read to the student a list of paired words—things like cat–dog, boy–girl, chicken–little, and the like. The teacher was then instructed to go back over the list and read the first word in each pair. The student was to select the second word from four choices. For each error made by the student, the teacher was advised to administer a shock by throwing one of the switches. He or she was to start at the lowest shock level and then move progressively up the voltage scale for each additional error. After explaining this procedure, the experimenter would use one of the following prods to encourage the teacher to continue: (1) "The experiment requires that you continue," (2) "It is absolutely essential that you continue," (3) "You have no other choice, you must go on," and (4) "Although the shocks may be painful, they will not cause permanent tissue damage."[2]

Starting with the first few errors, the student showed mild annoyance at the shocks. As they increased in voltage, however, his protests became louder. If the teacher continued to do what he was told, screams of pain and cries for mercy poured out from the student. The teacher, looking to the experimenter (authority) for direction or advice, received statements like, "While the shocks may be painful, they will not cause permanent tissue damage, so please continue the experiment." At 330 volts, after loud cries of pain and a complaint of a heart condition, silence is all that comes from the room of the student. The teacher, turning to the experimenter, is told that, "Silence will be taken as a wrong answer, please continue the experiment."

Although the people who played the role of teacher in the Milgram study underwent a great deal of personal conflict and frustration (an issue that has caused some to question the ethics of the experiment's design), the shocking results showed that approximately 60 *percent* of the subjects were fully obedient to the orders of the experimenter. More than half of the sample allowed their blind obedience to authority to override the shouts of pain and cries for mercy from the student. One subject, who thought he might have killed the student, was relieved to find that the experiment was a hoax. When later asked by his wife what he would have felt had the student died, he responded by saying, "So he died. I did my job!" If we define discipline as mere obedience, we can be pretty much assured that the Nazi prison guards at Dachau were not discipline problems.

Without some form of obedience, however, society could not function. Don Hamachek, a professor at Michigan State, has helped clarify this issue by making a distinction between rational and irrational obedience.[3] *Irrational obedience*, as he sees it, is the unquestioning obedience by which a human being can morally justify sometimes unkind or cruel behavior as simply "doing as told." Such people place the responsibility for their behavior in the hands of the authority. Conversely, *rational obedience* retains the essence of each person's ability or capacity to obey with discretion. He or she alone assumes the responsibility for his or her behavior. We all are occasionally placed in situations where if we don't do certain things we must experience the consequences. Knowing, however, that we have a choice is the difference between rational and irrational obedience. Often the choices are not easy. For the prison guard at Dachau, the choice was most likely his life or someone else's. It is difficult, however, to determine the consequences for disobedience in the Milgram study. All subjects were paid $5 at the beginning of the experiment and were told that the money was theirs regardless of the results. Disapproval from authority appears to be their only consequence—a phenomenon strong enough to cause more than half of the sample to override their personal conscience and responsibility.

Fallout from Obedience Training

For educators the issue is clear. Not only is it difficult to maintain a definition of discipline based on obedience, but we must also question the morality of such a definition. Our attempts to perpetuate such obedience training have contributed to the creation of a wasteland in our schools. I'm truly amazed at the large number of students who are slowly dying of boredom in our classrooms. We have always had students who disliked school, but I believe that this percentage is getting increasingly larger and that the "turn-off" is becoming deeper. Many are turning to alcohol and other drugs to relieve the frustration of this boredom. Twenty percent of my ninth-graders were smoking marijuana at least once a week, and twice that number were drinking beer, wine, and booze.

What scares me most is that the methods we are using to achieve our goals with these students may be producing results exactly the opposite to those we seek. For example, I think most educators would agree that we want students to learn to like learning—to receive a satisfaction from it. We know they will forget much of what we teach, but we want them to experience something valuable from the process, to develop skills of inquiry that will carry them into the uncertain future. In short, I think we can agree that we want students to develop a love of the learning process. Unfortunately, in trying to reach this goal, we are defeating ourselves in the eyes of many students. Instead of developing a love for learning, many students are beginning to despise it. We are inadvertently spawning an anti-intellectualism among a large percentage of students through a process of classical conditioning.

Reading is a good example. Many of my students who were

labeled "poor readers" knew how to read, but they had learned to hate doing it. I recall an eighth-grade student who was labeled as having a "reading problem." He told me he couldn't read; and when confronted with any printed matter, be it a page from a text, a newspaper, magazine, or handout, he made every attempt to avoid it. I could see the pain in his face whenever he was asked to read something. Nevertheless, I knew that he could read; I once saw him reading a lengthy note from another student. Unfortunately, as a result of the negative experiences this boy had associated with reading, he had learned to detest and loathe any contact with the printed page. You don't need great insight into the conditioning of Pavlov's dog in order to understand why such a process occurs. If you place persons in a situation that is frustrating and boring, they learn to avoid that situation. If a book or printed material happens to be associated with that situation, they also learn to avoid those things. I have heard that the average adult in today's society spends a mere five hours a *year* reading books. Certainly competition from the tube (which occupies about 1,200 hours a year) has much to do with this embarrassingly low figure, but I believe much of what we do in the schools has also contributed to it.

Many people believe the reason for our difficulties in school is that we are coddling the students, that we are too easy on them. They argue for the need to overpower and force students into compliance because in the long run compliance is better for them. My experience, however, has shown that the harder we push and directly force some students, the more they defy us. Such defiance may take the form of open rebellion, but most often it's passive resistance. Kids know that if they start to throw chairs around the room or openly talk back to the teacher, they're in real trouble. So, instead, many carry an air of smugness about them, which usually results in ignoring commands from the teacher or in showing a complete lack of involvement with and motivation to fulfill the teacher's wishes. I think this reaction among students is the reason that when teachers begin to talk about discipline problems, their conversation usually shifts to problems of motivation (an issue discussed in Chapter 3).

The frustration and disappointment I experienced during those first few weeks of my return to the junior high are still very vivid. I approached the undertaking with a great deal of confidence and belief that I could relate with the kids and even teach them some Social Studies. From their point of view, however, I was simply another teacher who was there to tell them what to do and when to do it. I was amazed at the reactions I received when I first tried to lead a discussion on urban problems with the ninth-graders. I had heard that junior high kids were a bit squirrelly, but I never imagined anything like this. They seemed to exhibit every behavior possible. Some were sleeping, others were out of their seats, some were playing tic-tac-toe, and one student was even pounding his head on his desk just to hear the noise it made. By making some outlandish statements on the topic, I was able to pick up a reaction or two from a few students, but the rest seemed to tune right out. They carried on their own conversations, poked each other, hassled each other by taking pens or pencils, and generally just screwed off. (While I did many of these things myself as a student, I don't remember being so blatant about it!) When one student made a comment on the topic, the others tuned out; when he finished, he tuned out, and someone else would tune in. As the bell rang I estimated that three-fourths of the group had not ventured a single word on the topic. What scared me most was that this topic was supposedly one of the "high interest" units.

From that day on, I developed a great deal of compassion for the problems of junior high teachers. I was eventually able to overcome most of the frustrations experienced by myself and by the students during those first few weeks, but the process was not an easy one.

A CHANGING GENERATION OF YOUTH

According to William Glasser, a major reason for our difficulties in education stems from a changing generation of youth in our schools.[4] His assumption is that students of today are different from those of the past. Students of the past (he uses World War II as the dividing line) viewed life from a completely different perspective. They, unlike the present generation, were goal-oriented; they were willing to subordinate themselves and their identities to the tasks or jobs that had to be done. While they may not have enjoyed studying or doing the work required in schools any more than present-day students, they realized that they must force themselves to do it anyway if they wanted to better themselves in society. The task, job, or goal was the overriding consideration; their identities or feelings of satisfaction came second. Glasser believes that children are no longer willing to subordinate themselves, their sense of worth, or their personal identities to the goals of the school. They seek reinforcement as persons, as separate human beings first, before they become involved with goals or tasks.

Yet schools, for the most part, are still goal-oriented institutions. If students work hard to achieve the goals of the teacher, they receive plenty of reinforcement that enhances their identities or sense of worth. Schools are very willing to provide such reinforcement, but the goals of the teacher and of the institution must be completed first. This conflict between role- or identity-oriented students and goal- or task-oriented schools seems to be producing the increased frustration of teachers and students alike. Teachers appear to say to the students, "The tasks, objectives, and goals of the class are really what's important. By reaching them, you will find your sense of personal worth and identity." Students, on the other hand, appear to say to teachers: "We want to find out who we are and be ourselves first, before we work for the goals you think are important for us."

The student's search for identity is not an easy road. It is often a very lonely, frightening process filled with disenchantment, particularly when support from families and schools is absent. The fact that the incidence of suicides among children under 18 years of age has tripled in America in the last ten years seems to attest to the difficulty of the search. During this search, the adolescent develops a heightened self-consciousness: Hairstyles, clothes, language, and music all reflect this consciousness. Neil Diamond's popular song of a few years ago that shouts out, "I am, I said, I am, I cried," or the one that says "I may be black, but I'm somebody," emphasizes the search. Much of the frustration of today's youth results from the conflict between this search and society's belief that what we *do* is more important than what we *are*.

The word "identity" is not as complicated as we are sometimes led to believe. Take away all the things that you do: What is left is what you are—your identity. To the extent that you see yourself as a worthwhile, lovable human being of some value, you can then begin to feel good about yourself and the people around you. I don't believe today's students are saying that goals are unimportant. They are, however, trying to say that what they are—their identities—are more important.

Moving from Goals to Identity

Some persons do not go through this search while they are in school. Instead, they allow the school and society to tell them who they are and what to do. At first, doing so looks easier. It involves less pain, and you needn't fight the frustration of uncertainty. Eventually, however, going this way catches up. For example, the 35-year-old "successful" businessman wakes up one day and asks himself who he is and what he's doing; he then quits his job and moves to a farm. In a sense, that businessman is just then experiencing *his* search for identity. A girl in my office a while back was in a similar situation. She had always, and without question, done what she was told to do. She studied hard to meet the goals of her school. Her parents told her to go to college and pursue a degree in teaching. Because this goal was comfortable and well accepted by society, she complied. As she was about to graduate, however, she found that jobs were not as available or as easy to get as she was led to believe. When it looked like she wouldn't get the type of job she wanted, she became quite upset. "How could they do this to me?" she shouted. She did exactly what she was told to do by her parents and school; she had subordinated herself to their goals, and now the payoff wasn't there. She was feeling very cheated and angry. After a few tears and a great deal of frustration, the experience eventually produced growth. For the first time in her life, she started to ask herself who she was and what she was doing. She was becoming identity-oriented rather than goal-oriented, and it was heartening to watch her begin to pick up the pieces and finally gain control over her life.

More students at earlier ages are beginning to make this shift. Three factors seem to account for the change.[5]

First is a *new sense of affluence* in society. People are beginning to believe that everything is okay, and they're not going to starve. "If I quit school and work in a factory, I can make plenty of money to provide for my material needs. If I can't find a job, welfare or Washington will carry me through. Since someone will take care of me, I may as well be concerned about myself rather than merely attempting to survive or earn a living." I was having lunch in a local tavern a few months ago and overheard one of the old-timers say, "What we need is another depression to shape these kids up. Let 'em feel what it's like to be hungry, and they'd soon cut out all this damn nonsense." There's no question that he was right: "Man lives by bread alone when there is no bread." Give plenty of bread, however, we begin to search for ourselves.

A second factor for the change can be traced to an *increase in political enlightenment* throughout our society. Human rights are valued and protected more than ever. A rich man is no longer worth more than a poor man, at least in a legal sense. Blacks, women, gays, and others all demand recognition as human beings, and many are receiving it. Some argue that the shift has been too slow. Nevertheless, since World War II, we, as a society, have become much more conscious of the value of human integrity, and we are beginning to do things to preserve it.

Television is a third factor contributing to the shift from goals to identity. The happy endings typical of most programs constantly hammer home the message that everything is all right. Any problem, regardless of the severity, can be solved in an hour, in between fifteen or twenty commercials. National advertising, in particular, perpetuates and exploits this concern with identity. Rather than discussing ingredients or costs, products are sold in terms of what they can do to make you a better person: "Use our product, it will make you feel better, more popular, more well liked." You need only observe a current toothpaste commercial to verify this process.

If Glasser is right that such a shift is taking place, we can better understand why a traditional approach to discipline, based on fear and coercion, is becoming increasingly ineffective. Many students simply are not scared enough to subordinate their identity—their sense of personal and social selves—to the tasks or goals of the teacher or school. The rewards or reinforcements offered by teachers are simply not strong enough incentives to do so. Further, if the student has little respect for the teacher as a person, then the conflict becomes intensified and can end only in frustration for both. Many argue that a large percentage of students are still doing well in school; they continue to find value in fulfilling the tasks and goals of their teachers. For the most part, however, these students are not doing so out of fear or coercion. They have developed a sense of confidence in their identities; they feel good about themselves and view the tasks and goals of school as further reinforcing this feeling. These students are goal-oriented, not because they have been coerced but because they have discovered that they can further enhance the positive feelings they have about themselves.

The problem is not that the goals and tasks of schools are unimportant, nor is it that they should be relegated to an inferior position. On the contrary, formal education has always been a most lucrative avenue for self-enhancement. Nevertheless, we cannot continue to rely on a system of discipline and instruction that requires the subordination of self to these goals. If we truly believe that education is self-enhancing, then we must design our instruction and environment to allow students to discover the school's potential for self-enhancement. Many discipline problems in the classroom might well be considered symptomatic of this underlying frustration between goal-oriented schools and identity-oriented students. Students who are involved in what they do and who, more importantly, find personal value in it, rarely act out and create disturbances. However, when we place persons in a situation in which they view what they are doing or what they are supposed to be doing as of little or no value to their lives, they naturally reject that situation. Either they act out this rejection by fooling around to provide stimulation, in which case they are labeled discipline problems; or they withdraw by falling asleep or by going to the Walter Mitty world of fantasy. Such behavior is not necessarily limited to students in school. You need only observe some faculty during inservice meetings to verify this phenomenon.

A HUMANISTIC APPROACH TO DISCIPLINE

It is becoming impossible in today's society to maintain a definition of discipline based on irrational obedience. To continue to do so can only result in undesirable consequences for our institutions and youth. If we truly want to effect a change in the present situation, then we must begin to define and view the concept of discipline as a process of developing internal controls. Since people are not born with such controls, discipline must be viewed as a learning process. More specifically, *discipline* may be defined as a process of maintaining order by helping students to discover the value, utility, and necessity of obeying reasonable rules and procedures, and to assume responsibility for their own behavior. Such a view of discipline is optimistic. It is based on a learning experience in which students examine the necessity for rules and procedures, explore the implications and consequences of their behavior, and, most importantly, assume the responsibility for it. Viewing the nebulous concept of discipline as a learning process might well be labeled a humanistic approach as opposed to an authoritarian one.

Unfortunately, some teachers who use a humanistic approach to their classroom problems end up with an unhappy situation: The kids are running all over them. The teacher is frustrated, the students are frustrated, and the behavior problems have doubled. For these teachers, the fine line between humanistic teaching and permissive teaching has not yet been discovered. They erroneously believe that a humanistic approach to discipline means becoming pals and buddies with their students, letting them do whatever they feel like doing, and generally staying out of their way and smiling a lot, even if they don't feel like it. It doesn't take long for these teachers to discover that chaos and bedlam result. Frustrated and disenchanted, many revert to cracking the whip and using the old techniques that they somehow survived with in the past.

It is crucial that we as teachers understand the distinction between humanism and permissiveness. For me, *humanistic teaching* means, first, being friendly and courteous to students at all times, regardless of how they treat us. It's easy to be friendly to students who are themselves friendly and do what is asked. Yet the students who are angry, detached, cold, aloof, and bitter also desperately need to be treated with kindness and warmth. I don't believe that, as teachers, we have the right to allow ourselves to treat these students as they treat us. If our goal is to help them with a learning problem (discipline), then we must be stronger than they are. By no means is this an easy thing to do. Many times we find ourselves becoming angry and disgusted with a student, and we find it difficult to be friendly and polite. With my eighth- and ninth-graders, I found it easier to avoid such negative feelings by constantly reminding myself that the student had the problem. One student, particularly, was able to get me upset a couple of times. He probably would have been able to get me more upset, had I not kept in mind that he was the one who was messing up and who needed my help. He had some serious behavioral problems. When I tried to view him as someone who needed help in learning the value of following rules and procedures, I didn't get as angry and disgusted every time he screwed up.

Secondly, I believe humanistic teachers must view their students as separate, unique human beings whose lives are much more important than any subject matter we have to teach them. The implication is not that what we are teaching is unimportant, but rather that the self-concept, individuality, and humanity of a student takes precedence over anything academic we have to offer. We can only hope that what we are teaching will reinforce a feeling of worth in our students; if it doesn't, then we must question what we are teaching. The issue is not so much that teachers value the humanity and worth of their students (I think most probably do), but rather that students regard teachers as behaving with this belief. Discussing this with a group of high school juniors, I recall a bright, articulate girl who believed that most of her teachers were much more concerned about the work she did than they were about her as a person. If she did her assignments and didn't ask too many questions, her teachers treated her nicely. If she missed an assignment or questioned the reason for having to do something that she felt was of little value, most of her teachers appeared cold and aloof toward her, did not listen to her concerns, and generally made her feel worthless. "They don't care about me," she said, "they only care about what I do."

A third factor in humanistic teaching is that we give students some voice and input in their education. We need not turn over our schools to students, but we must allow them some input in what they are going to learn, in how they are going to learn it, and in the rules and procedures necessary to bring about learning. We may, on occasion, have to overrule a desire of a student, particularly when it conflicts with the rights of others; but our willingness to hear and to accept their desires as real ones for them can do much to bring about a sense of cooperation and involvement.

Finally, I believe we must show students the same respect we would like them to show us. Often I hear teachers complain that their students simply do not listen to them. When they say something to a student, it seems to go into one ear and out the other. While this lack of respect can be nerve-racking, I wonder how many times we do the same thing with their comments. We can no longer simply tell students to, "Do what I say, not what I do." Students demand to be treated as equals. Their demands have nothing to do with equal background, experience, or knowledge, for they are well aware of such differences, but they do ask for the same respect, concern, and dignity that we, as teachers, seek.

I would like to emphasize that nothing in this philosophy is permissive; nothing says that we should abdicate our control over the class or that we should let students run wild and do whatever they please. Reasonable rules, procedures, and requirements are necessary in the classroom; and, as teachers, we have the responsibility and the obligation to help students carry them out. Erroneously, some teachers, parents, and even students view humanistic teaching as a sign of weakness. This usually happens when the distinction between humanism and permissivism is not understood. Humanistic teaching is not at all contradictory to firmness; permissive teaching is. When we say to students that we cannot permit them to continue to disrupt the class, we have to mean it. The way we deal with the problem, as emphasized in Chapter 5, is based on the student's motive and on the restrictions of the environment. Yet deal with it we must. Not with bitterness, but with firmness.

To disruptive students, their behavior has purpose and meaning. Let's take two examples:

Sidney is a student in Mr. Gordon's eighth-grade social studies class. He has been doing C work in the course, but, unfortunately, he has provided a constant headache for Mr. Gordon. Sidney is like a jumping jack, continually out of his seat, checking the weather outside, teasing the girls, doing his Fonzie and Incredible Hulk imitations, or "helping" Mr. Gordon keep order by shouting at the others to pay attention. He's not a cruel or destructive student; in many ways he's quite likeable. Nevertheless, his clowning around seems unending, often forcing Mr. Gordon to administer stern reprimands. Sidney usually stops his antics when Mr. Gordon blows up, but ten minutes later he's right back at it. Occasionally Mr. Gordon sends

2

THE CAUSES OF DISRUPTIVE BEHAVIOR
(how can they be so inconsiderate?)

Sidney into the hall to settle him down, but Sidney seems to get into more trouble out there, roaming the corridor and entertaining anyone who cares to watch. Mr. Gordon has kept Sidney after school to talk about his behavior, but it doesn't seem to help. Sidney apologizes for his behavior and promises to stop his fooling around, but a day or two later he acts as though he has completely forgotten the conversation. Others in the class find Sidney's behavior entertaining at times, but more often they see him as being overbearing and a showoff.

Matilda is a student in Ms. Jones' eighth-grade math class. She has never done well in math and has developed a strong dislike for it. She does, however, get good grades in her other courses. She is exceptionally talented in art, and is co-editor of the school newspaper. Because of the school board's concern for a return to basics, Ms. Jones takes a firm, no-nonsense approach to the teaching of math. She follows the textbook page by page, has daily homework assignments and weekly tests, requires that the students memorize all formulas, and sternly reprimands anyone seen with a calculator or mentioning the words "Texas Instruments." Matilda has been doing D and F work throughout the course and lately has been spending much of her time passing notes and talking with her friends. Ms. Jones is upset with Matilda's talking because it interferes with the math lessons. When she tells Matilda to stop talking and get to work, Matilda complies. She is, however, so far behind in her understanding of math that regardless of how much she studies, she is always confused. One day while Ms. Jones was describing the procedure for calculating the area of a parallelogram, Matilda began talking softly to the girl next to her. Ms. Jones became very angry and demanded that Matilda close her mouth and pay attention.

If "disruptive behavior" is defined as any behavior considered by the teacher as interfering with maintaining a constructive learning environment, then it follows that Sidney and Matilda are both disruptive. In Sidney's case, we see a boy manipulating the class and the teacher in an attempt to satisfy a need for recognition and attention. Matilda's behavior, on the other hand, appears to be a response to the frustration she feels about math. Both students are, by definition, disruptive.

Their motives, however, differ. To understand the causes of disruptive behavior, we have to focus on the motives of those students who choose to disrupt. Such knowledge not only helps us understand the behavior of the student, it provides a framework to deal with such disturbances as well (Chapter 5). It also helps us prevent or reduce their occurrence (Chapter 3).

There appear to be two distinct divisions of disruptive behavior. The following table shows the motives and goals within each of these divisions:

DIVISIONS OF DISRUPTIVE BEHAVIOR

DIVISION I:
TENSION-REDUCTION DISRUPTIVE BEHAVIOR

Motive of disruptive behavior: *to reduce emotional tension*	*Goals: to relieve frustration, anxiety, boredom, fear, excitement*

DIVISION II
NEED-SATISFACTION DISRUPTIVE BEHAVIOR

Motive of disruptive behavior: *to satisfy personal needs*	*Goals: to attain attention, power, revenge, noninvolvement*

Division I or "Tension-Reduction Disruptive Behavior" has as its motive the reduction of emotional tension caused by the school environment. (I have already noted that, as teachers, we often do much to cause the disruptive behavior we hope to avoid.) Placed in a situation that creates debilitating levels of frustration, excitement, anxiety, boredom, or fear, *any* individual responds by (1) suppressing these emotions and withdrawing or by (2) acting out and disrupting the environment that creates these emotions. Matilda decided to reduce her frustration and boredom with math by talking to her friends.

"Need-Satisfaction Disruptive Behavior" in Division II results when an individual uses the school environment to satisfy a personal need. Unlike tension-reduction disruptions, which have their origins within the school environment, need-satisfaction disruptions originate from within the individual. Such disruptions result from attempts to achieve the goals of attention, power, revenge, or noninvolvement at the expense of the teacher or other students in the class. Sidney appears to be disrupting Mr. Gordon's class in an attempt to satisfy his need for attention from others. While it may be argued that Sidney's need for attention can be traced to frustrations within his environment, such as uncaring parents and the like, the distinction between tension-reduction disruptions and need-satisfaction disruptions is based on the *immediate goals* at the time of the behavior.

TENSION-REDUCTION DISRUPTIVE BEHAVIOR

Many of the causes of tension-reduction disruptions are beyond the direct control of the teacher.

Administrative policies or pressures, for example, can force the teacher to work in extremely restrictive situations that create adverse learning environments for students. I have heard of a principal who believes that learning takes place only in the classroom where students sit quietly with their hands folded neatly on their desks. There are also administrators who feel that teachers should solve every problem that arises in the classroom and offer no support for recalcitrant students. Such administrative restrictions cannot help but contribute to adverse learning environments that force many students to respond with disruptions.

Peer pressure is another factor. Frustration and anxiety resulting from peer group conflicts also contribute to tension-reduction disruptions. While the importance of peer group acceptance varies from grade level to grade level, rejection at any level can produce frustrations that are vented through disruption. Name-calling, bullying, and ignoring by peers contribute to such frustrations. Many teachers who have been able to establish a basis of rapport with their students individually often feel helpless when faced with such peer group problems.

Relations with peers can also produce emotions of excitement, thrill, or silliness, which have a tendency to disrupt the learning environment. The following is an example of disruptive behavior resulting from the reduction of these tensions:

Dawn is a student in Ms. Wilson's seventh-grade English class. She has been a very competent student and has never caused a discipline problem. After lunch on this particular day, Dawn and her best friend, Mary, were going to Dawn's locker to get her books for class. The two girls were standing in front of the open locker talking about the things that seventh-grade girls usually talk about (candy bars and boys) when Dawn realized that the bell for English class was about to ring. She closed her locker and was about to lock it when she discovered she couldn't find the lock. She quickly opened the locker and began a frantic search through the myriad of papers, books, and chocolate bar wrappers in an effort to find the lock before the bell rang. Mary started to help Dawn sort through the mess. Both girls were beginning to feel nervous and panicky, knowing that they would have to suffer the wrath of Ms. Wilson if they were late for class. The effort was beginning to look hopeless when Mary realized that Dawn had unknowingly been holding the lock in her hand during the entire search. After locking the locker, they realized how absent-minded Dawn had been and broke into a fit of laughter. Rushing to class it seemed that the more they thought about the situation the harder they laughed. They arrived in their seats just as the bell sounded. Dawn was doing everything in her power to hold the laughter back, but just a glimpse at Mary sent her into an uncontrollable giggling spree. Ms. Wilson had finished taking roll and was now trying to get the class started in a discussion of the previous day's assignment. As the discussion began, Dawn was now biting her lip in an effort to keep from breaking up. Ms. Wilson, sensing that something was wrong and failing to see the humor in Dawn's antics, asked her to please pay attention. A few moments later as one of the students was discussing the assignment, Dawn, catching Mary's eye, could hold it no longer and burst out in a loud roar. Ms. Wilson firmly reprimanded Dawn for the disruption and sent her into the hall as punishment.

From Ms. Wilson's point of view, Dawn was obviously disrupting the class. From Dawn's point of view, her behavior was a response to the excitement she was experiencing. Any teacher who has ever had a class of students on the day before Christmas vacation knows the existence of tension-reduction disruptive behavior.

Our choice of subject matter and our method of presenting it also contribute to tension-reduction disruptive behavior. When we place students in a situation where what they're doing or supposed to be doing is perceived as being of little or no value, they naturally reject the situation. This rejection may take the form of withdrawal, with a tacit agreement between the teacher and student of "don't hassle me, and I won't hassle you," or the student may act out this rejection and frustration by fooling around and creating disruptions.

It's impossible to devise a curriculum where everything students study has a direct bearing on their lives. Furthermore, such a curriculum is unnecessary. What is crucial is that students feel that *most* of what they do in school is of value *to them.* Students, as well as adults, do a lot of things for which they don't see immediate value if they believe that *most* of what they do contributes to their self-enhancement. While a paradigm for major curricular reform is beyond the scope of this analysis, I wonder if it's not too much to ask that students believe that most of what they do in classrooms has meaning to them rather than to the teacher. Much of what we teach in schools can have meaning to students. Unfortunately, we sometimes get so involved with teaching the content that we fail to teach the value of it. How many times have you heard students say, "Why do we have to study this?" Following is a list of some of our typical answers to this question, and the underlying messages conveyed.[1] (I am indebted to Barb Herlihy, a friend and colleague, for sharing this.)

"WHY DO WE HAVE TO STUDY THIS?"
1. *The fifth-grade teacher (or the high school English teachers, or the professors at the university) will expect you to know this. . . .* Listen, son, what I am saying is that, if I had my way, I wouldn't teach you this stuff at all. I just work here, you see, and I have to get along with the rest of the folks on the payroll. I can't have the fifth-grade teacher yelling that the kids don't learn anything in my room, so I am going to teach you what she thinks ought to be taught.

2. *Educated people are supposed to know this.* . . . Frankly, I don't think this will ever do you the least bit of good, but some people set great store by it, and if you want the social and financial advantages which may come to you through association with so-called educated persons, then you'd better have a speaking acquaintance with these things.

3. *It will do you good when you grow up.* . . . I know this doesn't mean anything to you now, and I don't blame you for wiggling in your seats. But you want to be "big folks" some day, don't you? Well then, you learn about the square on the hypotenuse and store it away in your mind, and some day, bingo! It will pop into your mind just when you need it. (Frankly, son, I have serious doubts about it, but that's what they always taught me, and I've got to motivate this lesson somehow.)

4. *This is good training for your mind.* . . . Frankly, I know you probably will never use this piece of knowledge, in either the immediate or the remote future. But here are some pretty good mental gymnastics, and if you can master them, you probably will be able to master something else which will make more sense to you. I really don't know why we don't work on the other things instead, but we've got to keep ourselves academically respectable.

5. *Your parents expect you to learn this.* . . . Don't ask me why you have to learn this. Your folks want you to take algebra, even though most of them haven't done an algebra problem since they left school, and I am hired to teach it to you. If I want to keep the paychecks coming, I am going to teach what the papas and mamas in the community want taught.

6. *It's the state law (or the course of study).* . . . Listen, kids, we really are in this together. I don't like to teach this any more

than you like to study it. If any of the Big Shots come in while we are working on this, try to show an intelligent interest. We want them to think we're doing what we're supposed to do, don't we? Somebody handed us this, and we might as well make the best of it.

7. *This will be in the examination on Friday. . . .* Now, we all understand the rules of this old school game. It isn't what you know that counts toward getting an education but what goes down in my little book, so I'm being a good sport and letting you know just what it is going to take to get the kind of marks you want in the little book. Furthermore, I know you kids well enough to realize that you won't waste your time on anything you think I might not check on, so let's understand each other right now. You're darned tootin' this is going to be in the examination on Friday.

8. *Unless you get this work in, I simply won't sign a slip for you to attend the game at Hillville Friday. Or you can't play basketball, or you can't be in the junior play, or you can't get out to decorate for the prom. . . .* Listen, son, I've got you where I want you. I know that you haven't the slightest interest in turning in a paper on "What 'Il Penseroso' Means to Me," but I think it is important or I wouldn't have assigned it. They tell me in the office that you have to have my signature to be excused for this trip. You know what the price of that signature is. Now get out of here and whip up a paper. I know it won't be any good, but you'll have gone through the motions.

Trying to provide an immediate answer to students' questions as to why they have to study certain material is usually futile. Most often the student really means, "I don't want to study this." If we can listen to those feelings and accept them as being real, then—

and only then—may we begin to help students find the value in what they're doing. (The following chapter deals with this issue in more detail.)

Finally, we sometimes create our own problems. A sizeable percentage of tension-reduction discipline problems are inadvertently caused by us, the teachers. Nagging, sarcasm, ridicule, unrealistic tolerance limits, and a host of other not-very-pleasant behaviors can create an environment that produces frustration, anxiety, fear, and boredom for students. For these students, overt disruptions are a normal response to such adverse environments. Talking about teacher-caused problems isn't easy. It's a personal issue: Few of us are willing to admit that our behavior might be contributing to the lack of discipline in our classrooms. Often, we want to put the blame on the students, on the parents, on the administration, on the curriculum, or, for that matter, on other teachers. While these factors might be the major cause of a particular student's disruptions, we must avoid being too quick to put the burden on others without first reflecting on our own behavior.

How do we, as teachers, create our own difficulties? For one thing, our reactions in response to one student affect not only his or her behavior but also that of the rest of the class. After reprimanding a talkative boy for not raising his hand, I recall the surprise an elementary teacher felt when two other students came to her after school and begged her not to scold *them* in front of the class if they made the same mistake. The issue was not being reprimanded— they believed he deserved as much. Rather, it was being embarrassed in front of friends, something we as adults would also feel strongly about.

We can also contribute to our difficulties when we allow ourselves to carry our egos on our shoulders. Often we let a student's remark become a personal affront to our integrity as a teacher: "How dare you use that tone of voice to me!" instead of, "I really get upset when you talk that way!" While these two responses appear similar, one shows a vulnerable and injured ego while the other shows a normal human feeling.

After being out late one Wednesday night, I found myself facing Thursday morning with little sleep and a head like Humpty Dumpty. Rather than disclose my condition to my eighth-grade class, I pretended to be my jovial old self. It wasn't long before Dom, the class clown, was getting under my skin. He had a strong need for attention, which we had previously discussed; and we had agreed that, when his behavior got out of hand, he would simply go to the small conference room at the entrance to the pod and work there until he felt he could return without disrupting. We had established a friendly relationship over the weeks, and, coupled with a great deal of positive attention, the agreement seemed to work well. At the beginning of the semester he was spending almost half the time in the conference room, but six weeks later an occasional trip was all he needed.

On this particular day he started off by grabbing a pencil from Janet, one of the quiet, shy girls in the class, and he persisted by poking and teasing her with it. Rather than simply motioning toward the conference room with my head, a cue we had previously agreed to, I yelled out something like, "Dom, I've had it with you! I want you to stop that fooling around right now!" While such a remark might work with some students, Dom also had a need for power in situations like this, and my anger seemed to kindle that need. Instead of doing what I demanded, he continued with the hassling as if he never heard me. At this point I blew up, went over to him, grabbed the pencil from his hand, and told him to go and sit in the vice-principal's office for the rest of the hour. As we stared at each other, it was apparent that my anger had elicited a great deal of hostility and resentment within him. A look of hate and vehemence shot from his eyes as he slowly turned and walked out.

During the time remaining in the period I thought a lot about my overreaction, and in the following period I was able to call him out of his English class to talk. As he sat there somewhat subdued, I apologized for yelling at him as I did and for not following the plan we had previously established. After a few seconds of silence he said that he was sorry for hassling Janet, that he was just having a bad day. I smiled as I mentioned how the day was going for me.

Dom's clowning around and attention-seeking behavior was a problem he was having. His anger and resentment at being overpowered was a problem I created.

We often cause students' tension-reduction disruptions. Consequently, it may be of value if each of us as teachers, administrators, or parents take time to examine our own behavior, determining the extent to which we may be contributing to the problems we hope to avoid. Are our rules reasonable? Do students have input in their development? Do they understand the purposes for them? Are our tolerance limits too rigid or too inconsistent? Do our voice and nonverbal expressions convey one message while we are trying to send another? Do we accept the needs and feelings of our students? Do we allow our egos to get in the way of the goal of helping? Do we help students discover the value of what we are teaching? It is not easy to ask ourselves such questions. It's even more difficult to find the answers. Maybe our students can help.

NEED-SATISFACTION DISRUPTIVE BEHAVIOR

The second major type of disruptive behavior occurs when individuals use the classroom environment in an attempt to satisfy their personal needs. Such disruptions do not occur simply by chance. In the students' eyes, their behavior is purposeful and meaningful, although the goals may not be necessarily conscious. Understanding the goals of this behavior is of value, because our handling of it should be based on the particular goal involved. Students who disrupt the class to satisfy personal needs really believe that the behavior is in their best interest, that it will provide social status or produce desirable results. If they didn't believe this, they wouldn't disrupt.

Understanding the goal of the student who is being disruptive helps us handle each case on an individual basis. Rudolf Dreikurs, who has written a great deal about maladaptive children, has classified the goals of maladaptive behavior into the four categories of (1) attention-seeking, (2) power, (3) revenge, and (4) inadequacy.[2] While Dreikurs does not distinguish between tension-reduction and need-satisfaction motives for disruptions, it appears that his classifications are concerned primarily with the latter. His classifications certainly help us see beyond disruption itself. Identical misbehaviors may often be motivated by different goals. Two students, for example, who are disrupting the class by whistling loudly may be doing so for entirely different reasons. One may be seeking attention while the other may be making a bid for power. The methods we use to deal with one will not necessarily work with the other. Our success with each will be partly a function of our awareness of the particular goal involved.

Maladaptive children might not even disrupt the classroom in the overt sense; their behavior may often be passive and take the form of withdrawal. Such behavior is typical of those placed in the category of inadequacy. Some students, however, might also select passive behavior in attempts to satisfy their needs for attention, power, or revenge. Shyness, stubbornness, or Gandhian passive resistance represents such behavior. Since most teachers are concerned with the active disruptive behavior that destroys learning environments, we will focus primarily on active behavior in the attention, power, and revenge categories. In the long run, passive behavior can be far more maladaptive than active behavior, as it is often characterized by deep feelings of hopelessness and despair. For this reason, even though the behavior may not be disruptive to the classroom environment, we will also focus on passive behavior represented in the category of inadequacy.

Attention

The most frequent goal of need-satisfaction disruptions is *attention-getting*. Many students are forced to establish their worth and acceptance as individuals through the affection or attention they elicit from others. If I asked you to close your eyes and think of a student's name, it would probably be the name of a student who fits into this category. Attention-seekers dominate most of a teacher's time. In addition to providing a constant headache for the teacher, the class clown, pest, and showoff have as their basic goal the attention they gain from others. Threats, punishments, and reprimands all serve to satisfy the need for attention that these children are seeking: They prefer this type of attention to being ignored. With younger students, the goal is usually to seek the attention of the teacher with these behaviors. As the child grows older, attention from the peer group becomes equally, if not more, important.

Rather than disrupting the classroom environment, some students may actually exhibit useful or constructive behaviors to satisfy this goal. The "teacher's pets" or the "hangers-on" who follow you around the classroom to show you how nicely they have done their work, may do so out of a dependency on the attention and approval from you, the teacher. These students generally do not create discipline problems, and many teachers find having them in a class quite enjoyable. After all, their basic goal is to please you. Nevertheless, these students suffer from a form of maladjustment, and they are really quite vulnerable. They have not yet developed a sense of self-reliance or a confidence in their own strength. Consequently, they are forced to continually seek approval from others to maintain their sense of worth and acceptance. If you don't give them the attention they demand, they feel lost and rejected. Some may even begin to do disruptive things in order to regain it. With attention-seekers, the attention may be either positive or negative; in either case, it satisfies their need.

As much as cooperative attention-getters can please the teacher, disruptive ones can be exasperating. They seem to be able to create a constant annoyance.

Such was the case with Jeff, a student in my ninth-grade Social Studies class. He was a little larger than most students his age and used his size to constantly torment and threaten others in the class. It was apparent that most of his antics were bids for attention. Upon entering the classroom, for example, he would usually go directly to the chalkboard and write some harassing little remark about any of a number of other students in the class. For the most part his remarks appeared innocent enough, things like, "Sue loves Tom" or "Cathie has a new boyfriend." He would, on occasion, get a little more personal with something like, "Linda is easy" or "Judy took a shower with her boyfriend." Needless to say, others in the class failed to see Jeff's humor, and short little arguments resulted. Not being able to ignore his notes any longer, I pointed out to him that he was making others angry and asked him to stop. This usually brought the desired results for the rest of the hour. The next day, however, he was right back at it. I tried to watch for him as he came into the class so that I could prevent the writing before it occurred. However, as soon as my back was turned or as soon as I was talking with another student, Jeff, like a streak, was to the board with his little news for the day. His remarks were usually centered at other attention-seeking students, who could use the opportunity as an excuse for their own little show. The more secure students would ignore Jeff's remarks.

It was difficult for me to really get angry at him for these antics, since his general disposition was rather friendly. He always had a smile on his face and would usually stop when I asked. Nevertheless, I was growing tired of the game we were playing and decided that I must try to find a way of stopping it. I knew that I had to provide ways for him to get the needed attention by doing acceptable things in class. In the long run I hoped to try to help him develop a sense of personal self-confidence and self-sufficiency so that he wouldn't need the constant recognition from others. Before I could do this, however, I had to deal with the immediate problem I was having with his nasty little comments on the board. After a restless night of evaluating several different approaches, the answer came to me in a flash. The next day, I watched Jeff out of the corner of my eye as he came into the classroom. Usually our game would start with my watching him very closely as he entered. That day I ignored him. He approached the chalkboard, looked around, and then walked over to one of his friends and began talking about something. Unfortunately for Jeff, he had nothing to write with because I had gathered up all the chalk before class. Continuing this procedure each day permanently solved this simple but pesty problem. While he could have brought in his own chalk or taken some from another class, he somehow never remembered to do so. I often wonder why it took me so long to think of such an easy solution.

Power

Some students seek more than attention. They also seek *power*, a second goal of need-satisfaction disruptive behavior. These students are more difficult to deal with than attention-seekers. The more emphatic or insistent a teacher becomes over an issue, the more these students respond with defiance or rebellion. The power struggle that ensues can become very disturbing. Of course, the students usually lose such struggles since teachers ultimately have more power at their disposal and can bring in the big guns when the struggle becomes too great.

For many power-seeking students, however, the struggle itself is reinforcing. Once we enter into such struggles, our relationship with the student usually deteriorates to the point where neither the teacher nor the student is the winner. The more we make a point of confronting such students with their behavior, the more they fight back.

Power-seekers have the ability to elicit a great deal of anger from teachers and adults, as they represent a direct challenge to authority. Many beginning teachers have met their demise at the hands of these students. If it's any consolation, their challenge is often not personal; it's usually directed at the role of authority that the teacher represents.

Revenge

As students continue ultimately to lose power struggles, they are forced to the third goal of need-satisfaction disruptive behavior—*revenge-seeking*. They say to themselves, "You got me in school today, but I'll get your car tonight." Revengeful behavior cannot help but deeply hurt the adult working with this student, and this hurt is often translated into a wish to retaliate or to get even, in which case a vicious cycle is created. These students evoke from us the type of treatment that further justifies their thirst for revenge, forcing us to retaliate again and again.

Revenge-seekers often generalize their revenge to all teachers, adults, and even to society. An example of this was related to me by a teacher in one of my classes. It concerned a high school math teacher who was walking through the hall in a large urban school. A student, whom the math teacher had never seen before, punched the teacher squarely on the mouth, knocking him down and loosening three teeth, which required dental care. Later, it was found that the student had been in a power struggle with his English teacher and was punished for his violence. As a result, he generalized his hate and revenge to all teachers, and the unfortunate math teacher suffered the consequences. The seemingly unbelievable wanton vandalism of beautiful art treasures, landscapes, books, or other fine things is often traced to individuals motivated by this goal. "You hurt me, so I'm going to hurt you," is what this person is saying. The "you" is generalized to include all society.

Noninvolvement

The fourth goal of need-satisfaction disruptive behavior is *noninvolvement*. Students attempting to satisfy this need hide behind a display of real or imagined inadequacy. Since their goal is to be left alone, their behavior is not necessarily disruptive, at least in an overt sense of the word. These students often internalize a feeling of complete discouragement and resign themselves to a life as a failure. "Since I'm no good and can't do anything right," these students say to themselves, "I may as well not do anything at all." It's as if these students were pounding their heads against a brick wall for several years—and then finally realize that it feels better to stop. Our attempts to have them do school work are usually seen as requests to start pounding again.

Many teachers find children who actively seek attention, power, or revenge the most trying, nerve-racking, and time-consuming. Yet they usually have more success in redirecting the behavior of those students than in motivating a passive, withdrawn student to participate actively. Such withdrawn students do not really create discipline problems in the sense of cutting up or acting out. Consequently, it's easy to lose them in the shuffle. Nevertheless, these students are probably the most maladjusted and, in the long run, need most of your help.

Understanding Need-Satisfaction Goals

Don Dinkmeyer and Jon Carlson have developed an "ABC System" for understanding misbehavior.[3] The following table shows an adaptation of their system to understanding the goals of need-satisfaction disruptive behavior:[4]

To utilize the "ABC System" for hypothesizing the goal or goals of a particular student, the first step is to observe what the student does (Column A). The second step is to examine what we do in reaction to the student's behavior and how we feel about it (Column B). The third step is to observe what the student does as a consequence to our behavior as noted in the second phase (Column C). By following this procedure, we can develop a better understanding of the goals of students who disrupt the classroom to satisfy their personal needs.

Students disrupt the classroom for various reasons. In some cases the behavior might be motivated to reduce the tension caused by the immediate environment. In others it might be motivated to satisfy personal needs. In any event, the methods we use to prevent or deal with the disruption must be based on an understanding of the motive or motives involved. In a sense, we must make a tentative hypothesis or guess as to the motives and goals operating and then act accordingly. Pinpointing the behavior, talking with the student, and looking at our own feelings all help in forming this hypothesis.

In some cases a particular child's behavior may act to reduce tension as well as to satisfy a need. Students, for example, whose inability and frustration with reading cause them to act out and disrupt in class, may also have a strong need for attention, which is being satisfied by acting out. To help them reduce the frustration and meet their needs, we must be aware of both motives. Failure to consider all the factors can only result in defeat for the teacher as well as for the student.

The Causes of Disruptive Behavior

ABC System for Understanding the Goals of Need-Satisfaction Disruptive Behavior

GOAL	"A" WHAT STUDENT DOES AND THINKS	"B" WHAT TEACHER DOES AND THINKS	"C" WHAT STUDENT DOES AS CONSEQUENCE OF "B"
Attention	Showoff; clown; thinks, "I only count when people pay attention to me."	Annoyed; reminds often; coaxes; reprimands; thinks, "This student takes too much of my time" or "I wish this student would not bother me so much."	Temporarily stops disruption when given attention.
Power	Stubborn; argues; disobedient; thinks "I must dominate to be of value" or "I only count when I do what you want me to."	Challenges student– feels provoked and angry; thinks, "You're not going to get away with this. I'll show you who's running this class."	Escalates power struggle when challenged or reprimanded.

Revenge	Vicious; defiant; thinks, "My only hope is to hurt others as I feel hurt."	Wants to retaliate; feels deeply hurt or outraged; thinks, "How can this student do this to me?"	Tries to get even; tries to hurt others.
Noninvolvement	Withdraws; gives up; rarely participates; feels hopeless; thinks "I am no good and since I can't do anything right, I won't do anything at all."	Throws up hands in despair; thinks, "I can't do anything with this student."	Passive; no reactions since student does not disrupt and is not reprimanded.

The following examples should help distinguish between tension-reduction and need-satisfaction disruptions. Read through each example and try to make a tentative hypothesis as to the motive of the student. If the motive is personal need-satisfaction, determine if the goal is attention, power, revenge, or noninvolvement. Assume you are a visitor sitting in the back of the room of a typical ninth-grade Social Studies class.

EXAMPLE 1
As the students come into the room, a boy named Eric takes two pencils and sticks one up each nostril pretending he is a walrus. As one of the girls walks by, he makes a loud bark in an attempt to scare her. Others tell him to stop fooling around, but as he takes his seat, he keeps waving the pencils and laughing.

Tentative hypothesis of Eric's motive—

EXAMPLE 2
As the teacher begins to get the class started, Jana is looking through one of the reference books in the corner of the room. She has a reputation of being a discipline problem and appears to have a very bitter attitude toward school and teachers. As she pages through the reference book, you happen to catch a glimpse of her writing obscene words with red ink on one of the pages.

Tentative hypothesis of Jana's motive—

EXAMPLE 3
The teacher begins to get the students working on an assignment from their text. Don, a poor reader, has been quiet and paying attention. He begins the assignment along with everyone else but after ten minutes he gets out of his seat and starts walking around the room. He is reprimanded by the

teacher for his behavior and is told to return to his seat and to do his work. He returns to his seat and tries again. After five minutes he purposely breaks the lead on his pencil and quietly goes to the pencil sharpener to sharpen it.

Tentative hypothesis about Don's motive—

EXAMPLE 4

Paula is a transfer student from another state. This is her third week in class. Last week the Social Studies teacher started the four-week unit of the Civil War. Paula had finished a five-week unit on the same topic at her other school. When she told this to the teacher, he explained that it would be best for her to work along with the rest of the class because he has no idea of what they had covered at the other school. She had begun the assignment from the text, but after ten minutes, she started a conversation with the boy next to her. Soon they were giggling and laughing.

Tentative hypothesis of Paula's motive—

EXAMPLE 5

Jerry, a very angry-looking boy, slouches around in his chair trying to find a comfortable position. He gets up and goes to the door. It looks like he's going to leave, but he changes his mind and goes to the pencil sharpener. After sharpening his pencil about ten times, the teacher asks him to get away from the sharpener and return to his seat. He responds by saying, "I just got here, and I need to sharpen my pencil."

Tentative hypothesis of Jerry's motive—

EXAMPLE 6

Tina plans to quit school next year and become a "go-go"

The Causes of Disruptive Behavior

dancer. She is well developed for her age and will probably be very successful. Throughout this unit she continually asks the teacher why she has to study the Civil War. She sees no value in it for her life. Today, rather than doing her assignment, she walks over by a group of her friends and starts to do the "bump" to some imaginary music. They seem delighted with the performance and encourage her to continue. The teacher sternly tells her to return to her seat. She returns but continues her little dance on the way. Most of the class seem to love it, and many applaud her when she's finished.

Tentative hypothesis of Tina's motive—

EXAMPLE 7
Leslie walks into class without saying a word to anyone. She takes her seat when the bell rings. She has done very little work all semester. When the assignment is given, she takes out her book but does not open it. As she is staring out the window, the teacher tells her to get started on her work. She opens her book to the wrong page and then stares at her desk.

Tentative hypothesis about Leslie's motive—

ANSWERS
EXAMPLE 1: Eric appears to be the class clown. If this is the case, the disruption would be motivated by need-satisfaction, and his goal is attention.

EXAMPLE 2: Jana appears to be seeking revenge by defacing the book. Her behavior is motivated by need-satisfaction; her goal is revenge.

EXAMPLE 3: Don's motive appears to be tension-reduction. His inability to read makes the assignment frustrating, and he walks around the room to relieve his tension.

EXAMPLE 4: *Paula's motive appears to be tension-reduction. Her boredom caused by going over the same material again is relieved by talking to the student next to her.*

EXAMPLE 5: *Jerry would probably get into a power struggle with the teacher if given a chance. His behavior appears to be need-satisfaction rather than tension-reduction, and his goal is power.*

EXAMPLE 6: *Tina's behavior seems to be both tension-reduction and need-satisfaction. She is bored with the curriculum but also seems to crave the attention of her friends.*

EXAMPLE 7: *Leslie is not being disruptive. She appears to want to be left alone. Her motive is need-satisfaction, and her goal is noninvolvement.*

One frequently hears the complaint from parents and teachers that psychologists and university professors are overly theoretical and too philosophical when it comes to problems of discipline. What good are their $10 theories and stoical insights, the argument goes, if they can't be directly translated into techniques for dealing with students who disrupt. While sympathizing with this complaint is easy, two pitfalls must be avoided when trying to delineate a specific course of action for dealing with a particular problem.

First, since no two students are ever identical, their reactions to a specific disciplinary procedure will never be identical. No blanket solution can be guaranteed to work with all students. For example, a book written for parents and teachers gives solutions to hundreds of indexed discipline problems: If you have a problem with a student throwing spitballs, fighting on the playground, or playing with matches, all you have to do is look up the misbehavior in the index

3

PREVENTING DISRUPTIVE BEHAVIOR

(a gram of prevention is worth a kilogram of cure)

and turn to the page that tells you what to do about it. By following the recommended procedure, you solve your problems quickly and simply. At first glance this technique appears to be a useful and straightforward approach.

Unfortunately, however, many teachers complain that universal solutions given do not work with their particular problems. Although they carefully follow the recommended procedure, the students do not respond the way they are "supposed to." I recall a student teacher who was having difficulties with a boy throwing spitballs in class. According to the procedure recommended in the book, she was to arrange for the student to come in after school and throw a large number of spitballs at a target on the wall, picking them up and counting them each time. The purpose of this procedure was to satiate the student with the disruptive activity so that he would no longer have a desire to continue it when he returned to class the next day. According to the example in the book, this method worked very smoothly and completely solved the problem. Unfortunately for the student teacher, her spitball-throwing student did not respond the way the book indicated. As recommended, she kept the student after school, explained the situation and then set up the target on the wall. At this point, however, the student refused to play the game. The student teacher again explained what he was to do, but the student just sat there. Unprepared for this turn of events, the student teacher became flustered. She and the student were having a first-class power struggle, and it was apparent that the student was winning. When it became evident that she could not make the boy throw the spitballs, she gave him a lecture on his bad behavior and allowed him to leave. Two days later the student was again throwing spitballs in class.

Despite many similarities among the problems we deal with as teachers and parents, students fight or throw spitballs for different reasons. Some may seek the attention of the teacher by their behavior. Others may be challenging the teacher to a battle for power. If we are to be successful in helping these students change their behavior, then we must consider the emotions and motives operating in each case. No one method, approach, or technique works with all fighters or all spitball throwers.

A second difficulty with the "solution" approach to discipline is that no two parents or teachers áre ever exactly alike in disposition or personality. Consequently, when you are dealing with discipline problems, no one technique or method works for all parents or teachers with all students. Parents and teachers differ just as students differ. The approach used with any problem must be a function of the personality and beliefs of the teacher as well as the emotions and motives of the student. Failure to consider any of these variables can only result in a hit-or-miss approach to resolving problems.

While some may consider this view theoretical or philosophical, it need not be impotent. By understanding ourselves and the motives of students, we can indeed translate these considerations into specific plans of action.

The disruptive behavior diagram discussed in the previous chapter assumes that disruptive behavior is a function of the needs, emotions, and environmental factors influencing a particular student at the moment of behaving. It follows, then, that individuals working to prevent disruptive behavior must concentrate on those environmental factors which they can directly influence. Specifically, teachers have control primarily over their own behavior. To the extent that their behavior produces emotional responses that are vented through disruption by the student, teachers have the control mechanism to prevent those disruptions. Similarly, parents have preventive power over those emotions for which they are contributing factors. As teachers, we do not have direct control over parents' behavior, nor do parents have direct control over teachers' behavior. While we can sometimes influence all the enviromental factors, emphasis in this chapter is on those behaviors under our direct control.

To understand the effects of environmental factors on the emotional responses of disruptive students, we must make a concentrated effort to see the environment from the point of view of the disruptive student. If we want to understand why children disrupt, then we must try to see the situation from their eyes rather than ours. All behavior—yours, mine, and little Johnnie's who throws erasers at his teacher—is the result of how we see ourselves in the situation with which we are involved. We all see ourselves in many ways, as teachers, as parents, as graduate students, as banjo players but not singers, and so on. The total of all these ways of seeing ourselves psychologists call the *self-concept*. To prevent classroom disruptions we must try to appreciate children's self-concepts.

We must do so, because both tension-reduction and need-satisfaction disruptions are often caused by students who are lonely and discouraged, and who have developed a failure or negative self-image. They simply do not see themselves as worthwhile, successful human beings who are doing things of value. Students who view themselves this way may decide to act out their failure identities by saying to themselves, "If I'm going to be a failure, I may as well be a good one." When you say to this student, "John, this is the fifth time I've told you to stop fooling around," he says to himself, "Well, he's getting to know me. I'm becoming the best troublemaker in class." Others may handle their failure identities by resigning themselves to their inferior status and by giving up or withdrawing. "Just leave me alone and let me sleep or daydream," seems to be their motto. Such students are usually not disruptive, but they certainly are in need of help.

In preventing disruptive behavior, therefore, the first step is preventing students from accepting and internalizing such negative views of themselves. This sort of prevention comes under the direct influence of the teacher or parent working to help the child, if we understand the child's self-concept. As a teacher, I have direct control over the things that I do to influence such identities. I cannot control what parents and others do, but I do have control over my own behavior.

To understand how our behavior influences the development of such negative self-concepts, it may be beneficial to examine the factors that contribute to a positive self-concept. Why do some students feel good about themselves in school, see themselves as successes, and cause few problems? Two major factors appear to characterize lives of successful students.[1] First, students with a successful self-concept or positive identity have experienced a sense of being loved or cared for. Love is a difficult word to define, but in this context the essence of its meaning conveys a relationship where one individual regards another individual as a separate, unique human being, and is concerned and involved in that person's existence. Usually this feeling is instilled in early life by loving parents, but many of us have experienced the feeling through our relationships with brothers, sisters, uncles, aunts, grandparents, close friends, and even teachers. The second factor is the belief that what students do is of value to them. We may call this characteristic a sense of worthwhileness, a feeling that what I do is worthwhile to my life. This feeling need not be continuously present. We are obligated to do many things in our daily lives that we may not find of value or consider worthwhile. Nevertheless, our sense of positive identity depends on the balance scale of worthwhile versus valueless experiences. Only when our personally involving experiences outweigh the mundane ones can we feel successful.

These two dimensions, love and worthwhileness, comprise the foundation of preventing classroom discipline problems. The first dimension can be considered in terms of teacher–student relationships. My belief is that the prevention of disruptive behavior has its genesis in this dimension. The second dimension can be considered in terms of motivation and relevancy.

TEACHER–STUDENT RELATIONSHIPS

Involvement

The key to improving teacher–student relations can be found in an understanding of the word "involvement." We may define this word as a feeling of love, caring, friendship, unconditional positive regard, or any of a number of other terms. Regardless of definition, the term implies that one person is truly concerned about another person, as a unique human being, whether he succeeds or fails, whether or not he picks up his clothes, or whether he's a good reader or poor. Persons who experience such involvement know that the "significant person" gets angry or upset when they leave their clothes lying around, when they don't do their assignments, or when they're late for an appointment. Yet they also know that, regardless of their behavior, the "important" individual still cares for them and has faith in them as human beings. Inherent in the concept of involvement is the belief that individuals' present lack of skills in no way diminishes their value and worth. Not only is such caring important to the development of students who succeed in school, but it is also crucial to the existence of our democratic society. Only when people really care for other people can they begin to care for themselves, and only when people care for themselves can they begin to care for others. Such is the interdependence of society—like it or not, we need each other.

Many of us as teachers are fearful of becoming involved with students. Somewhere during our training we either assumed or were told that teachers shouldn't become involved with students. They should remain detached and objective. Unfortunately, such aloofness has not only widened the communication gap between teachers and students, it has hamstrung our efforts to help students become self-disciplined. Occasionally, teachers equate the word "involvement" with "entanglement." There is a distinction between the two terms: While some teachers may become entangled with their students, I believe it is the *lack* of involvement that is most prevalent in our schools. *Involvement* is based on caring and helping; *entanglement* is based on meeting our own need to be liked at the expense of our goal of helping.

Since involvement is such a difficult concept to translate into teacher behaviors, it may be helpful if we view it simply as the process of making friends with students. Again, we must be careful not to equate friendship with becoming buddies or pals. I assure you, a 12-year-old doesn't need a 35-year-old buddy. The word "friend," however, implies something different. Most of us have at least one friend, and looking at the characteristics of that relationship might be of value. Why do we call some people our "friends" and others "acquaintances"? When we carefully examine our relationships with individuals whom we classify as friends, one factor seems to stand out from the others. I believe the major characteristic of a friend is that he or she *listens* when we share a concern. Friends convey to us a genuine interest in our problems and a willingness to give of their time. Often friends merely serve as sounding boards for us to bounce off our thoughts and feelings. In this process we become free to explore and clarify our beliefs and concerns. Through the dynamic process of actively listening, friends help us to understand ourselves better. Rarely do friends ridicule, preach, moralize, or threaten. When they do, we usually no longer view them as friends.

Most teachers honestly care for their students. They have devoted their professional lives to helping students, and they want their students to leave at the end of the year feeling knowledgeable, confident, and successful. Ironically, this is exactly what most students also want for themselves. Therefore, while it is important for teachers to care, it is equally important to the process of developing positive self-concepts that students *believe* that their teachers care.

Unfortunately, I've seen many cases in which teachers honestly care for their students, but the students see exactly the opposite. It's important that we care and have faith in our students, but it's equally important that our students believe we care. The following is an example of such a situation:

Paula is a ninth-grade student in Mrs. Wilson's English class. Since the beginning of the year she has been a good student, but lately she has not been doing her work, has been talking quite a bit during class, and has been sending notes to one of her friends. Stopping her after class one day, Mrs. Wilson initiates the following dialogue:

MRS. W: *Paula, you haven't handed in your assignment again today. You know if you continue with this behavior, I'm going to have to give you a D for this grading period.*

P: *Yeah, I know.*

MRS. W: *Not only are you not doing your assignments, you're disturbing the rest of the class with your talking and sending notes while others are doing their work.*

P: *I'm not talking any more than the other kids. Why are you picking on me?*

MRS. W: *Now don't start talking back to me, young lady. I'm not talking about the other kids in class, I'm talking about you. I want that talking in class to stop or I'm going to have to call your parents.* [Paula is silent.] *You have the ability to get an A in this class, Paula, and you're really letting me, your parents, and yourself down if you don't work up to that ability.* [Paula is silent and looking at the floor.] *Usually I don't accept late work, but because you have the potential to be a good student,*

I'm going to give you until Friday to get in all of your late assignments. You're going to have to stop disturbing others, though, or I'll still have to call your parents. [Paula is still silent and looking at the floor. Her eyes are beginning to water.] Do you understand what I'm telling you, Paula?

P: Yes.

MRS W: Good, you can go now. But remember, I'm expecting to see a change in your behavior. [Paula leaves.]

The next day Paula is quieter than she has been previously and even hands in part of one assignment. As the week progresses, however, her behavior deteriorates, and she fails to hand in more work. Mrs. Wilson calls Paula's mother to tell her of the problem, but it doesn't seem to make much difference in her behavior.

The teacher in this example honestly wants what's best for Paula. By doing her work, getting an A, and paying attention, Mrs. Wilson believes that Paula will become a happy, well-adjusted, successful person. Paula, however, sees only a teacher who is interested in assignments, grades, and noise, and who really doesn't care about her as a human being. Even if Mrs. Wilson had specifically told Paula that the purpose of the discussion was to help Paula become a happy, successful person, chances are that Paula would not have believed her.

The following is an example of another teacher, Mrs. Smith, working with the same problem.

MRS S: Paula, I'm concerned about some things I see happening in class. You haven't been handing in your assignments lately, and I've noticed a lot of noise coming from your area. What seems to be the problem?

P: *There's no problem.* [Paula replies quickly.]

MRS. S: *You just don't seem to be yourself, lately, Paula. You seem to be nervous and tense, and I have the feeling that something's upsetting you. I don't know if I can help, but I'd like to try. Can you tell me about it?*

P: *There's nothing you can do.* [Mrs. Smith is silent, and Paula continues.] *I guess there's nothing anyone can do, except maybe Sue. She sits next to me in your class, and she's my best friend. I don't see her all day except for this class. We have different lunch schedules and ride different buses. I guess that's why we have been talking so much in here.* [After a long silence, Mrs. Smith responds.]

MRS. S: *It's pretty important to you that you have a chance to talk with Sue?*

P: *Uh-huh, she's the only one that understands.* [Paula's eyes begin to water.] *You see, Mrs. Smith, my parents are going to get a divorce, and I don't know what to do. I haven't told anyone because I'm so ashamed. I don't know what's going to happen to me and my brother.* [Paula begins to quietly cry.]

MRS. S: *It's awfully frightening not knowing what others will think or what's going to happen. It sounds like Sue has been the only person you could turn to for help.* [Paula stops crying and wipes her eyes.]

P: *Yeah, her parents were divorced last year. She really is able to understand. That's why it's been so important for me to talk with her. I know it's been disturbing the class and I haven't been doing my work. Do you think you could help me change my lunch period so that we could eat together? I really like your class and want to do well, but it's just been so difficult not having anyone to talk with.*

MRS. S: *I'm not sure what I can do about your schedule, Paula, but I would be happy to talk with Mrs. Olson, our guidance counselor, about it. Would you like to come with me, and explain the problem to her?*

P: *I've wanted to talk to her about my parents before, but I've been afraid. I think it would be easier if you would come with me.*

Later that week Paula begins turning in her past assignments.

While this example could be used to demonstrate differences in communication skills between these two teachers, its primary purpose is to show differences in caring and involvement. Both teachers are involved with Paula. Yet only in the second example, however, does Paula believe the teacher cares about her as a separate, unique human being.

Authenticity

In addition to involvement, *authenticity* is a second factor important to the development of effective teacher–student relationships. An occupational hazard of our profession is to lose the uniqueness of ourselves and to respond, after a while, according to stereotyped roles of teachers. The function of colleges of education is to prepare teachers. Unfortunately, some graduates become so involved with the role of a teacher that they forget their own identities as human beings. After a year or two in the classroom, they find themselves saying all the things that their own teachers said to them, things they though they would never say.

Students cannot identify with teachers—they can identify and become involved only with other human beings. We get a feeling for this reaction when we observe students reacting to teachers in nonschool situations: They are often amazed to see their teacher in a supermarket or movie theater. "You mean you go to movies! You go shopping! Man, you're a schoolteacher. They don't do those things!" A pregnant teacher really blows their minds, not because they don't know where babies come from, but because schoolteachers are different. They're not supposed to do human things. When we hide behind the role of teacher and disguise our own humanity and individuality, students have a difficult time identifying with us.

I recall the words of my daughter after she returned home from her first day in first grade. As we were having dinner I asked her about the people she met at school. She said, "Well Dad, Mrs. S is the first-grade teacher, Mr. W is the P.E. teacher, and Miss C is the art teacher. The bus driver's name is Joe, and he's really neat!" Joe happened to be ten years older than any of her teachers; but because his name was Joe rather than "Mr." or "Mrs." something or other, she could identify with him. Using titles or first names is not the issue here. What is important is that we allow our humanity to come through, regardless of what we're called. Fortunately, my daughter had very good teachers, and in time she was able to relate with them as human beings. Nevertheless, as teachers we do have first names. Why are we afraid to let our students know them? We also have the same needs, anxieties, and frustrations as other human beings. Why are we obsessed with hiding them? How often have we found ourselves in situations where a student says or does something hilarious in class, and we say something like, "That's enough now, Billie; let's get back to work"—only to find ourselves in the lounge later having a big laugh about it, as we share the incident with the other teachers? Why are we afraid to laugh about it with Billie?

Another problem when we hide behind the role of teacher and do not share ourselves is that many students become confused about the messages we send. For example, the teacher with a headache or hangover walks into class and says, "Okay, let's keep it quiet in here! I want everyone to sit down and get to work." Usually, ten minutes later, when the noise level returns to normal, her head is killing her, and she begins screaming and shouting. The students view the teacher's shouting as unfair since they are only acting the way they normally act. I made this mistake with Dom and my eighth-grade class, as related in the previous chapter. Perhaps I should have said something like, "Class I have a splitting headache and I would appreciate it if you could hold it down" or, "Take it easy today, kids, teacher's worn out." Maybe the students might have identified with such human conditions and responded accordingly. I do not mean to imply that we should use our classrooms as places to "bare our souls," but a little humor and honesty with feelings can go a long way in improving teacher–student relationships and preventing disruptive behavior.

Power and Authority

A third factor affecting teacher–student relationships is the teacher's use of power and authority in the classroom. As a function of our positions as teachers, we are given authority over students. We then convert this authority into power through the use of rewards and punishments. Those teachers who view discipline as the process of obedience training rely most heavily on the use of these rewards and punishments to maintain their authoritarian stature. Some students actually prefer authoritarian teachers and do quite well in their classes. For the most part, either these students are excited by the content of the course, or they find personal meaning and satisfaction in doing the assigned task, or they may be quiet, docile, passive students who prefer the security in being told exactly what to do and when to do it.

A sizeable percentage of students, however, respond with defensiveness and rebellion to the use of power. These students cause teachers to rank "lack of discipline" as their number-one national concern in education today. These recalcitrant students simply will not do what they're told, and the rewards and punishments we have available just will not make them. As an alternative, some teachers give up trying to use their power and authority and allow the kids to do as they please. Outwardly they smile a lot and try to be buddies and pals with the students, but inwardly they begin to resent themselves as well as the students. As Herbert Kohl has so eloquently put it, "We find ourselves becoming either dictators or doormats."

EXPLORING THE MIDDLE GROUND

Most conflicts between teachers and students stem from conflicting needs. For example, assume that two students are chitchatting during Mrs. Williams' eight-grade Math class. Mrs. Williams has a need to keep these students quiet so that they and the others can learn about solving equations. The two students, however, have a need to talk to each other about the dance on Saturday night. Such a conflict can be resolved in one of three ways.

First is the authoritarian approach, based on power. In this case, Mrs. Williams demands silence from the two students and will use any form of punishment available to enforce it. Staying after school, detentions, lowering grades, and going to the principal's office are punishments commonly used for this purpose. The scenario usually starts with a request, then a demand, followed by a threat, and finally a punishment. Something like, "Sue and Donna, please stop talking and get to work on your assignment." The results of this request are based on the previous relationship between Mrs. Williams and the girls and on the strength of their need to talk about the dance. If the relationship is good, but their need strong, the girls usually stop for a minute or two while Mrs. Williams is staring at them. If the relationship is poor, they may simply continue to talk. In either case, when the talking continues or starts up later, Mrs. Williams reverts to step two, the demand. "Now I want you two to stop talking and get to work!" Again the effect of the demand is based on the quality of the relationship and on the strength of the need. If the girls continue to talk, Mrs. Williams escalates to step three: "Now that's enough girls! If I have to tell you to stop talking again, you're both going to have a detention!" The effect of the threat is now based not only on the relationship and on the strength of the need to talk, but also on Mrs. Williams' previous history of carrying out her threats and on the deterrent effect of detentions. If the talking continues, Mrs. Williams has no choice but to assign the punishment and/or offer threats of more severe consequences.

The second approach involves more permissiveness. If Mrs. Williams is a permissive rather than an authoritarian teacher, she probably never gets beyond the first stage of making requests. She might say something like, "Sue and Donna, will you please not talk so loud." She hopes the girls will stop and do some work, but she's also reluctant to *insist* that they stop, for fear that they may become angry. As the talking continues, which it usually does in permissive classrooms, Mrs. Williams feels frustrated and upset, but outwardly she ignores the girls and allows them to continue.

Obviously, there must be some form of control within a classroom. Without it we have chaos. Rules and regulations are necessary for classrooms to function as learning environments, and the teacher's responsibility is to maintain this order. The word "control," however, implies a form of order or authority based on the social system of the classroom or school. The purpose of the control is to maintain the social order and the learning environment. Power, on the other hand, is often used to enforce the personal needs of the teacher rather than the social order. When used in this manner, the needs of students are sacrificed to meet teacher demands. Consequently, resentment and disruption usually follow.

As mentioned in the first chapter, a third approach lies in the middle ground between authoritarianism and permissivism. Call it what you will—"democratic" or "humanistic"—the distinguishing feature is that it is based on neither personal power nor abdication. In the first example, the authoritarian Mrs. Williams relies on power to meet her needs at the expense of the needs of Donna and Sue. Given enough power, established through effective punishments, authoritarian teachers can satisfy their needs or win such conflicts, while the students lose. Even though the teacher's needs may be based on the student's best interest, relationships founded on personal power widen the gap between teachers and students by developing resentment on the part of the losers. Dependency, fear, and lack of responsibility are similar by-products. With the permissive Mrs. Williams, Donna and Sue are able to satisfy their need to talk and thus win the conflict at the expense of the needs of Mrs. Williams. In this case, Mrs. Williams experiences the resentment, anger, and frustration—and ends up the loser. In either the authoritarian or permissive case, there are winners and losers. Unfortunately, resentment on the part of the loser produces only a widening of the gap between teachers and students.

Contrary to the authoritarian and permissive approaches, the humanistic approach is based on the mutual satisfaction of needs. Although doing so is not always possible, the teacher makes every effort to resolve the conflict without a winner or loser. The success of this effort is contingent on opening a two-way communication between teachers and students. This communication is characterized by (1) teachers' listening skills that permit and encourage students to express and explore their needs and concerns, and (2) confrontation skills that allow teachers to express their needs without injuring the relationship. Simply stated, these skills help teachers listen so that students will talk, and help teachers talk so that students will listen. (The following chapter deals with these skills in detail.) The purpose of the skills is to resolve conflicts without satisfying the needs of one individual at the expense of another's. Such mutual satisfaction requires that both teacher and student explore and share their needs, try to understand each other's concern, and attempt to work out an agreement that is satisfactory to both.

Neither the authoritarian or permissive Mrs. Williams makes an attempt to understand the needs and concerns of Donna and Sue. Furthermore, neither expresses her needs and concerns in a way the girls can understand and accept. The humanistic Mrs. Williams might deal with this conflict by starting with an expression of her own concern. Something like, "Donna and Sue, your talking to each other when I'm trying to explain this lesson is frustrating for me because you're missing the information, and I don't have time to go over it again." Mrs. Williams has described the undesirable behavior (the girls and her trying to talk at the same time), her feelings about it (frustration), and the problem it creates (not being able to explain the instructions again). She has given neither a command nor a threat, but she has merely described the situation and her feelings.

As with authoritarian or permissive statements, the effects of such a statement will be based on the previous relationship between Mrs. Williams and the girls and on the strength of the need for the girls to talk. Assuming a previous relationship of respect and understanding and assuming that the need of the girls to talk is not too strong, they will probably stop. They were most likely not aware that their behavior was causing a problem for Mrs. Williams. On the other hand, if the girls have an important reason or strong need to talk with each other, they might well express it at this point. Donna might say, "But Mrs. Williams, I haven't had a chance to talk with Sue all day, and she has to catch the bus right after class. We have to decide something about this weekend." At this point the needs of Mrs. Williams and the needs of the girls have been expressed.

Arriving at a mutual solution to such a needs conflict is not easy. If Mrs. Williams allows the girls to continue to talk, she does not satisfy her need. If she demands that they stop, the girls do not satisfy their need. A solution demands a willingness of both parties to examine alternatives that permit each to feel satisfied. In this case the two girls could possibly get their work done first, and then at the end of the period take a couple of minutes to talk. If Mrs. Williams passes Sue's house on her way home, she might be able to drop her off, allowing the girls time after school when they could talk. Maybe Donna could call Sue on the phone in the evening. Maybe the girls could go into the hall for a couple of minutes and get the directions from a friend when they returned. Some of these solutions sound better than others, but it's important that a solution be found to which both Mrs. Williams and the girls can agree.

Many argue that teachers do not have the time to deal with such conflicts in this manner. Some say that the teacher's needs are more important than those of students. Others are concerned with the effects of this method on the remaining students in the class. In response to these concerns, I believe it important to emphasize that the purpose of resolving conflicts through mutual needs satisfaction is to improve and enhance teacher–student relationships. When both teachers and students believe that their needs will not be sacrificed to the whim and power of the other, good things happen. Teachers and students begin to work together in mutual concern for each other. Fewer disruptions occur, and less time is wasted with power conflicts. A sense of reasonableness prevails, where both teachers and students begin to feel good about themselves and what they do. Occasionally teachers may be forced to use the power that goes with their authority, but I believe that as needs are mutually satisfied, the teacher–student relationship gets better and the discipline problems become fewer.

MOTIVATION AND RELEVANCY

While a humanistic orientation on the part of the teacher can do much to prevent some types of discipline problems from arising, most teachers are quick to point out the apparent high correlation between discipline problems and the lack of motivation in their students. I believe it's a mistake to assume that students are not motivated. We are all motivated; every human being, regardless of background, has the basic fundamental motivation of seeking self-enhancement. It's hard to believe sometimes that the grisly boy in the back row, who has not done a bit of work all semester, is seeking self-enhancement; but we must remember that from *his* point of view, his lack of involvement in the class seems to be the most appropriate thing he can do. If he believed he had a more appropriate option, he would certainly take it. From our vantage point, his behavior may appear to be self-defeating. We must constantly remind ourselves that people behave according to how they see the world, not how we see it. While we may believe that all students should know the four reasons for the spread of Christianity in the Roman Empire, many may not agree with us.

Closely related to the concept of motivation is the concept of relevancy. While this term has become overused, I believe it also is misunderstood. We make a great error when we arbitrarily assume that the content of what we teach is relevant or irrelevant. We cannot say that the reasons for the spread of Christianity in the Roman Empire are either relevant or irrelevant. Each of us must decide that for ourselves. If I enjoy reading and studying about historical facts, the Empire might be very relevant for me. If I have absolutely no interest in the Roman Empire at the stage of my life that it is presented, then it probably is irrelevant to me. However, getting a good grade on my history exam might be very important to me; in this case, the spread of Christianity in the Roman Empire becomes relevant to that particular purpose.

Relevancy is a function of personal motives and purposes. Many students are no longer willing to learn facts and information just to get good grades. They are beginning to demand that what they learn must have meaning for their lives. One high school teacher told me that when she asks her students what they want to learn, the answer is usually "nothing." Many of her students do not believe that "things" learned in high school have a relationship to their present lives. After all, learning what to do or not do in the back seat of a station wagon is not usually in the curriculum. When we cannot find direct relationships between our curriculum and students' lives, then we must rely on the inner satisfaction that comes from achievement for its own sake. We have all experienced the pleasure and fulfillment that springs from a self-motivated effort. If our curriculum does not have direct relevancy to the lives of our students (most do not) then we have little choice but to try to "hook" student interests and curiosities. Unfortunately, when students are forced to sample *all* content—whether they like it or not and when they must spend most of their lives in school answering questions rather than asking them—they soon forget these curiosities. Take a look at little kids before they get to school. They seem to have an unlimited store of questions to be answered by adults. Whenever I took a ride in the country with my daughter, I groped for the answers to questions like, "Where do cows come from?" or "Why do some cows have brown spots, and others have black spots?" Somehow, kids learn that the ground rules change when they get to school. Instead of seeing teachers as people to provide answers to their questions, they quickly learn to provide answers to the teacher's questions. Maybe, because they become so busy answering those questions, they soon forget how to ask their own. I recall a line I once read a number of years ago that has always stayed with me: "The fatal error in education is that we throw answers, like stones, at the heads of those who haven't yet asked the questions."

Both relevancy and motivation must be viewed from the eye of the individual. Consequently, one of the most difficult problems faced by teachers is how to select, structure, and present their expertise in a way that helps and encourages students to find their own personal value in it. Students must believe that what they are doing in school contributes to their own self-enhancement. It is easy for us to tell them that; but unless students discover this from their point of view, our advice has little effect. Of course, all of us do many things that we find to be of little personal value, whether it's taking out the garbage or solving simultaneous equations. Our decision to do those things, however, is based on a belief that *most* of what we do is in our best interest, and these not-very-valuable tasks enable us to maintain an environment that contributes to our self-enhancement.

TEACHER EXPECTATIONS

Another phenomenon that has contributed to our difficulties in schools is the self-fulfilling prophecy in classrooms. When we allow ourselves to believe that students are going to be a discipline problem, chances are that they end up that way. Our expectations have the effect of becoming realities. Rosenthal and Jacobson have substantiated this phenomenon as it relates to academic success. Their book, *Pygmalion in the Classroom*, has far-reaching implications for teachers.[2] They went into a large California school system at the beginning of the year and told the teachers that they had developed a new test called the "Harvard Test of Inflicted Acquisition." They built it up to be the greatest breakthrough in standardized testing since Binet; and, of course, everyone was impressed. They continued by telling the teachers that the test would identify students with latent potential who were about to do things the coming year—"spurters," they called them. After the test was administered, each teacher was given the names of five students from his or her class that the test had identified as "spurters." Unknown to the teachers, the test was nothing more than an old standardized intelligence test, and the names were randomly selected from each teacher's class list. Rosenthal and Jacobson returned at the end of the year and again tested the students with the same intelligence test. Sure enough, they found that those students randomly identified as "spurters" did, in fact, "spurt." Significant increases in IQ were found between the "spurters" and the control group.

If we expect students to do well, they do. An interesting finding of the study was that when they interviewed the teachers to determine what they had done differently with the "spurters," many could not even remember the names of the students so identified. Evidently, the changes in IQ were the result of small subtleties of which the teachers were not consciously aware.

While this study was criticized because of its research design, teacher expectations certainly appear to be a factor in student performance. While no data confirms the conclusion, I believe that when we expect students to behave as discipline problems, many of them do. I recall reading the Rosenthal and Jacobson research during the late sixties, when activists were breaking into draft offices and burning draft records. I couldn't help but think that if I were a bit more subversive, I would have broken into principals' offices throughout the country. Instead of burning the cumulative records, I would have added twenty points to each student's IQ. It would have been interesting to see the results.

THE FALLACY OF HORSE SENSE

Finally, I believe the "fallacy of horse sense" has also contributed to our difficulties in school. An example of this faulty reasoning is when we believe that the way to produce responsible, decision-making behavior in students is to make all their decisions for them. We fail to realize that self-discipline is no easy task and can be learned only in situations that allow individuals to experience the consequences of their own behavior. There certainly are limits as to how far we go here, but we must consciously build in opportunities to allow students to assume the responsibility for their own behavior.

Another example, based on the opposite line of reasoning, is when we believe that experiencing failure in school is the best way to prepare students for the failure that is so much a part of the "real world." Research on frustration tolerance show us that exactly the opposite happens, at least when it comes to coping with frustration.[3] If one of the signs of a fully functioning adult is the ability to tolerate frustration, then—following this line of reasoning—we should make a conscious attempt to frustrate our students when they are young. After all, we must preapre them for "life." We could give little Johnnie an ice cream cone and when he's really into it, take it away from him. When he begins to scream and cry, we can tell him that we are only helping him to learn to tolerate frustration and that when he becomes an adult, he will thank us for it. Fortunately for little Johnnie, our research shows us that exactly the opposite happens. Those people who were found to have the highest levels of frustration tolerance as adults, experienced the least amount of frustration as children. We must be careful not to allow "horse-sense" fallacies to determine our actions with children in school.

If we view discipline as the process by which we help students learn the value and necessity of following reasonable rules and procedures, then we must constantly examine these rules and procedures, as well as why some students have difficulties following them. We must continually examine ways to help students learn the necessity of such limits, and we must scrutinize approaches for dealing with overt problems that result when some have not yet mastered this learning. Many of our actions and reactions as parents and teachers inadvertently contribute to our discipline problems. Likewise, there are a percentage of students whose favorite indoor sport is hassling teachers. There are no absolutes in this process. Approaches and limits vary from teacher to teacher, just as motives and needs vary from student to student. Hopefully, by examining the approaches used by teachers and the motives influencing students, we can cut sticks of self-confidence, understanding, compassion, and firmness, to replace those made of hickory.

When problems occur in the classroom, teachers and students must get together and work them out. They have no choice. Dialogue is necessary, and the nature of this dialogue is the concern of this chapter.

"When I talk to a student it goes in one ear and out the other" is a complaint often heard from teachers. "I tell the student how he's screwing up and what he can do to change, but it's as if I'm talking to a brick wall!" When we confront such students with their lack of obedience, the response is usually a shrug of the shoulders or silence. It's easy to see why many teachers yearn for Friday afternoons.

Before we are too quick to condemn the student as the culprit, it may be of value to examine our own tendency to build brick walls.

4

TEACHER – STUDENT DIALOGUE

(it's like talking to a brick wall!)

How often do we really hear what students are saying to us? We may listen to the words, but do we really understand their feelings and concerns? If we don't, can we really expect them to respond differently to us? I've seen students so frustrated by adults not hearing and understanding them, they have given up trying to express themselves. Furthermore, these students have learned that given about seven seconds of silence, many teachers answer their own questions. The teacher's monologue often goes like this:

Suzie, I called you in to talk about your behavior in class today. What's the problem? [Silence and Suzie looks at the floor.] *You know you have been fooling around and not paying attention. What are you going to do about it?* [Silence and a shrug of the shoulders.] *Well, you had better stop it and start paying attention, or I'm going to have to have a little talk with your parents.*

The teacher in this example may feel relieved for having "talked" with Suzie, but it's apparent that the conference will have little effect on Suzie's behavior.

Students, also, find silence uncomfortable. Rather than suffer the agony, many have discovered that the classic response of "I don't know" usually brings the same results. They may or may not know the answer to the teacher's question, but they can be fairly certain that if they say they don't, the teacher tells them.

Breaking down brick walls between teachers and students requires a two-pronged attack: First, we must examine ways of talking so that students listen; second, we must examine ways of listening so that students talk. In the first situation we have a problem with students' behavior, and we want them to know about it. In the second, our goal is to help students explore their problem or concern.

CONFRONTING WITHOUT INJURING

As a teacher, the behavior of my students is either acceptable or unacceptable to me, depending on my standards and expectations. Suppose, for example, that I expect my students to request permission before leaving their desks. If Bella is out of her desk without my permission, then obviously her behavior is unacceptable to me. I may choose to ignore her, or I may confront her. In any event, *I* have the problem—Bella's behavior is unacceptable. It is important to realize that *I* own the problem, not Bella. While her behavior may be the cause of my problem, it is still my problem—not hers. Likewise, if I'm giving a lecture on the Westward Movement, and Bella finds my behavior boring, then *she* owns the problems, not I. While my own behavior may be the cause of her problem, it is still *her* problem—not mine. This distinction as to who owns the problem is crucial to understanding the nature of teacher–student dialogue. Thomas Gordon, in his book *Teacher Effectiveness Training*, gives a detailed analysis of this concept of problem ownership. [1]

When a student's behavior is destructive to the learning environment, we as teachers initially own the problem: The student's behavior is unacceptable to us. While we may temporarily ignore it, in the long run we must confront the student with our problem. If our sole purpose is simply to stop the inappropriate behavior, our confrontation is most often characterized by ordering, directing, commanding, threatening, warning, moralizing, advising, persuading, criticizing, name-calling, or even ridiculing. If we have enough power behind us, such confrontations usually achieve our goal. In doing so, however, these messages also tend to elicit other reactions.

Suppose, for example, you are a student of mine in one of my classes at the university. I have a standing rule for the class that only one person talks at a time. Suppose, also, that during my "exciting" lecture on problem ownership, you were carrying on a discussion with the person next to you about the merits of collective bargaining. Since I had the floor first, you were clearly in violation of my rule. Your behavior is unacceptable to me, and, accordingly, I own the problem. If my sole purpose is to solve my problem by stopping your disruptive behavior, I might give you a request ("Please stop the talking") or a command ("I want you to stop talking right now!"). If I were in a particularly bad mood, I might give you a warning ("You had better stop talking if you know what's good for you") or a threat ("If you don't stop talking out of turn, you're going to flunk this class"). I might also start moralizing ("You should know better than to talk while I'm talking") or criticizing ("You are really impolite to talk when I have the floor"). If I were nursing a headache, I might even resort to sarcasm ("You with the bionic mouth, stop trying to steal the show!").

If my objective is to stop your disruptive behavior, my guess is that any of these statements would produce the desired change. In doing so, however, I'm sure they would also create many other feelings and reactions on your part. The anger, hostility, embarrassment, resentment, bitterness, or humiliation you might feel would certainly affect your attitude toward me, the course, and yourself.

Approaches to Confrontation

Three factors should be considered when confronting students about their unacceptable behavior. First, the method of confrontation should have a high probability of stopping the undesirable behavior. While the behavior may not stop immediately, the confrontation should set the foundation for finding an amiable solution. Second, the confrontation should not destroy the relationship between the teacher and student. Winning the war is of little value if you lose the peace. Only by maintaining and strengthening the relationship between teacher and student can long-lasting changes occur. Finally, our style of confronting should avoid injury to the student's self-esteem. Most disruptive behavior is caused by students who see themselves as failures. Further reinforcement of this view of themselves can serve only to perpetuate "undesirable" behavior. In the preceding example, my methods of confronting you for talking in my class satisfy only the first criteria—stopping your undesirable behavior. The effects of these confrontations on our relationship and on your self-esteem are obvious.

The following are characterizations of some typical approaches to confrontation. Assume you are a tenth-grade Science teacher. As you are explaining the concept of barometric pressure, Johnnie, a short, cocky little fellow, gets out of his seat, starts wandering around the room, eventually goes over to one of his cronies, and begins a conversation. You might ask yourself if the following confrontation styles meet our criteria.[2]

1. THE GENERAL: *Johnnie, sit down and be quiet!* The General gives commands and orders, and expects them to be obeyed. This sort of teacher knows exactly what the student should do and sees no need to give explanations or to listen to the student's concerns. Power and fear are usually required to make the student carry out the orders.

2. THE HISTORIAN: *Johnnie, this is the fifth time you have been out of your desk this period!* Historians confront by throwing students' past behavior back at them. In a sense, they imply that students should not only change their present behavior, but they should also reform their past—a very difficult assignment. The General and Historian often work together.

3. THE SWAMI: *Johnnie, if you don't stop talking and go back to your desk, you're going to get an F in this unit!* The Swami likes to predict the future. Whenever you hear a threat, you hear

the swami. Like the General, the Swami relies on power and fear to scare students into changing their behavior.

4. ZORRO: *Johnnie boy, if you took a bath more than once a month, you wouldn't have ants in your pants.* Zorro is an expert at cutting up students in front of others. The sword-like sarcasm or ridicule is sharpened to a fine point and usually produces a red face on even the toughest hombre.

5. THE REV: *Johnnie, you really should be more considerate of others in here.* Revs are preachers by trade. They moralize about the student's inability to live a virtuous life. While the rhetoric sounds good, it has little effect on Johnnie. The Rev can increase effectiveness by preaching at self rather than others.

6. THE JUDGE: *Johnnie, for being out of your seat, you will stay ten minutes after school.* The Judge dispenses punishment. Coupled with the judgment is a rational explanation to show students how their behavior has caused the crime. Unfortunately, little is done to rehabilitate the criminal. The "hanging judge" seems to be the most feared.

The effects of these six typical confrontation styles on the teacher–student relationship, self-concept, and behavior of the student cannot be directly predicted. The teacher's personality and previous relationship with the wandering student, as well as the student's motive for wandering, all need to be taken into account. Nevertheless, if the teacher's habitual response to disruptions is characterized by the General, the Historian, the Swami, Zorro, the Rev, or the Judge, it is likely that: (1) the relationship between the teacher and student will deteriorate, (2) students will develop negative views of themselves and (3) the undesirable behavior will continue or, at best, be reduced only temporarily. To test this assumption, put yourself back into the shoes of a high school student. What feelings did you experience when you were ordered around, threatened, or embarrassed by the teacher? If you were fortunate enough to never have experienced these confrontations, how do you imagine your friends felt?

Some argue that, although threats, orders, or commands are not popular, they occasionally stop the inappropriate behavior. To understand why this happens, go back to the model for the causes of disruptive behavior presented in Chapter 2. The effects of any confrontation are a function of the teacher–student relationship and the motive of the student. If the behavior is attention-seeking, then such confrontations serve to provide that attention and most likely stop the behavior temporarily. However, if the behavior is power-seeking, confrontations characterized by the General or the Judge serve only to escalate the conflict. Since the General and the other five friends have the potential for eliciting self-defeating reactions, we must examine other methods of confronting. For confront we must—to ignore is to invite chaos.

As an alternative, we can make confronting more effective if we focus on ourselves rather than on the student's behavior. The six villains previously described share an emphasis on students and their behavior. This emphasis does little to tell the student the nature of the problem experienced by the teacher. The teacher has the problem—not the student; therefore, it's up to the teacher to let the student know the nature of the concern. To demand that the student change without knowing what the teacher is feeling or experiencing is too much to ask. Students simply aren't buying it. Self-disclosure by the teacher is the key: We must let students in on what's happening inside us. Disclosing our feelings to students is difficult and risky. Furthermore, there are no guarantees that the behavior will change even after we have done so.

The following example may help clarify this issue. Zelda, a freckled-faced fifth-grader, is out of her seat during most of her reading class, talking endlessly to anyone who cares to listen. Finally, she kicks over the wastepaper basket. By this time her teacher is most likely experiencing a problem. One way to view the problem is in terms of the emotional reactions it creates. Most teachers would probably experience annoyance, frustration, or anger at Zelda's behavior.

Take Mrs. Murphy, Zelda's teacher, for example. She tries all morning to get her Bluebird reading group to follow along while each takes a turn at reading a sentence from the SRA Book-of-the-Week. She doesn't particularly enjoy the task, but in the back of her mind is the gnawing realization that standardized reading tests will be given in her school the following week. At the last faculty meeting her principal spoke for two hours about the importance of these tests. Unfortunately, the Bluebirds were not in attendance at the meeting and find it difficult to get charged up over this week's story about Dick and Jane's new horse. It was just as Dick was saying, "Oh! Oh!" for the seventh time, that Zelda wiped out the wastepaper basket. While Mrs. Murphy is a gentle, caring teacher, it is easy to understand how she could be transformed, like Captain Marvel, into the General, the Swami, or the Judge.

The frustration and anger experienced by Mrs. Murphy are normal emotions felt by many teachers. Denying or suppressing these feelings can result only in more frustration, phoniness, or a nervous breakdown. What follows is a way for Mrs. Murphy to vent these feelings without injuring her relationship with Zelda or injuring Zelda's self-esteem. Furthermore, this approach should have a high probability of changing Zelda's behavior.

"I-Messages"

Thomas Gordon has coined the term "I-message" to describe a method of confronting others that avoids the pitfalls of the typical confrontations discussed previously. Simply stated, it is a confrontation composed of (1) a nonjudgmental description of the unacceptable behavior, (2) the feelings experienced as a result of the behavior, and (3) the concrete effects of the behavior. The formula used to construct such messages is: "When you _____, I feel _____ because _____."[3] In Mrs. Murphy's case, the formula would be something like "Zelda, when you walk around the room and kick over the wastebasket, I feel angry and frustrated because it interferes with our completing today's story." The theory behind I-messages is easily understood. It is Gordon's belief that I-messages maintain the relationship between the teacher and student, do not injure the self-esteem of the student, and increase the likelihood of behavior changes.

In practice, however, I-messages are difficult to use. When I discuss the method with my class at the university I find most teachers agree with Gordon's ideas. Unfortunately, when they begin to use the approach in their classrooms, they experience frustration and often give up. There appear to be several reasons for this failure. First, the use of a formula for confrontation often makes the message sound mechanical and rehearsed. As one teacher said, "If I confront my ninth-graders with this, 'When you . . ., I feel . . ., because . . .' stuff, they look at me like I'm some kind of a nut!" Second, many teachers find it difficult to disclose their feelings with students, not only because it is sometimes difficult to find the right words to express these feelings, but also because they fear becoming vulnerable when they do so. Third, there seems to be a little voice in the back of some teachers' minds that says that they *shouldn't have to* tell students all this. If students are disrupting, they should be told to stop or punished—"I shouldn't have to tell them about myself." Finally, there seems to be a lack of faith in the ability of I-messages to stop or change behavior: "I confronted the student, as Gordon says, and he just ignored me and continued his talking" was a comment shared by another teacher.

Self-Disclosure

To avoid the mechanical nature of Gordon's formula, some of my students have found it more beneficial to disregard the term "I-message" and simply confront their students by disclosing themselves. While these confrontations may include the three elements of an I-message, the emphasis is on the internal experiences of the teacher and on sharing them with the student. If a student's behavior is driving us up a wall, we ought to tell that student exactly what we feel. This is no easy task. It requires two important and difficult prerequisites: (1) an awareness of the feeling we are experiencing, and (2) a willingness to take a risk.

The first prerequisite seems simple enough. After all, how could Mrs. Murphy, in our previous example, not be aware of the feelings she has about Zelda's behavior? She is obviously angry and frustrated. In addition to these surface feelings, however, we should also be aware of any underlying feelings involved. Anger is usually a secondary feeling generated by a more primary, underlying feeling. Ferreting out these primary feelings is not always easy, but it is necessary if we want more genuine, honest communication. In addition to the anger Mrs. Murphy is feeling, she also may be experiencing feelings of inadequacy with stopping Zelda's behavior, or a fear of being viewed by the principal as a poor reading teacher.

The second prerequisite to confronting by disclosing self is a willingness to risk sharing our feelings with the student or students involved. Whenever we open up our feelings with another person, we become vulnerable. The vulnerability is based on the belief that the person could use this information against us. If Zelda knows that Mrs. Murphy is feeling frustrated and inadequate, she may purposely continue her behavior to increase these feelings. This fear of disclosing, felt by many teachers, is often very difficult to overcome. I have experienced it many times. It's as if I were hanging from a cliff with my bare hands and someone was telling me to take the risk and let go. Whenever I have had the courage to do so, however, I've found that I only fall a couple of inches and, in a way I cannot explain, somehow end up on a higher plateau than when I started.

I shall never forget taking such a risk during my first year of teaching. I was working in a small rural high school at the time, and I was being harassed and intimidated by a junior girl in my second semester World History class. She was a popular student who did average work. Unfortunately, it seemed that her sole purpose in life was to make my first year of teaching as miserable as possible. Her behavior was not overtly disruptive. Rather, it was her snarling, hostile looks and venomous glares that caused me to think about going into the life insurance business. I had no idea as to the cause of her animosity. All I was sure of was my own misery. Day after day, I sat in the faculty lounge dreading the arrival of this seventh-hour class. My only respite was waiting each morning for the absence list in hopes that her name would be there. For some reason she preferred to sit in the front row. Consequently, I found myself conducting the class from the opposite side of the room. Whenever I looked at her or asked her questions, my knees shook as the hostility and vehemence spewed out. I would have been happy to trade her for Atilla the Hun.

After about eight weeks of this agony, I finally decided I could take it no longer. I had no alternative; I had to risk confronting her. I nervously mentioned to her one Friday that I would like to speak with her after school. I had no idea what I was going to say, but in the back of my mind I kept thinking that when all else fails, the only thing left is total honesty. Five minutes after the last bell she walked into the classroom, took her usual seat, and started glaring at me. My deodorant was being pushed to its limit as I went over and sat in the desk next to her. I don't recall the exact words I used as I began stammering about the reason I had called her in. I only remember that once I got started, the words came easy. I told her how much I disliked her behavior in the class and how happy I was when her name was on the absence list. I mentioned the frustration I was experiencing, and the nightmares I was having. I continued on for several minutes describing my lamentation, and, finally, when I had finished, I felt as if someone had just lifted an albatross from my neck.

My relief was short-lived, however, as she responded by venting her feelings toward me. She described how much she disliked the class and how happy she was when absent. She continued for several minutes and finally ended by saying she didn't like my behavior either. We both just sat there for awhile and looked at each other. The air had been cleared. Each of us had known for weeks how the other felt, but now that it was said out loud, face-to-face, the hostility and negativism seemed to be defused. I pointed out that two months were left in the semester and wondered what, if anything, we could do about the situation. Neither of us seemed to know where to go from that point. So I suggested that she tell me specific things I was doing that bothered her. I could try to change. This she did, and I was surprised by her comments. She was upset because I always stood on the other side of the room, seldom calling on her or talking with her as I did with some of the others in class. She was obviously right; but, rather than try to defend my behavior, I simply said I was sorry for doing it and I would try to avoid it in the future.

After a few seconds of silence, she then asked me to tell her what she was doing that made me so angry. I told her about the snarling glares that sent shivers down my spine, and we both chuckled. With this, the conference was ended. We agreed to try to avoid hassling each other, and she left. The following weeks were not always rosy, but we were able to peacefully coexist; by the end of the semester, we could actually joke and smile together.

In analyzing this confrontation, two factors seem to stand out. First I shall never forget how difficult it was for me to disclose to this student what I was honestly feeling. Her behavior made it obvious that she was aware of these feelings, but sharing them, face-to-face, was a difficult risk for me. The second thing that seems important—and I believe the reason for the confrontation's ending on a positive note rather than in a shouting match—was the way in which the feelings were shared. By chance rather than by design, I vented my frustration without attacking, criticizing, or blaming her for my feelings. I merely focused on myself, almost to the point of self-pity. In the process, however, she did not develop a need to defend or deny her behavior. This circumstance made it possible for both of us to accept each other's feelings, to find a workable solution, and, most important, to accept our humanness. In retrospect, the solution to our conflict seems simplistic. I believe this further emphasizes the value of improving teacher–student dialogue.

Disclosing your feelings to a problem student in a nonblameful, nonjudgmental way may not immediately stop the disruptive behavior. Nonetheless, the advantage of this approach centers on its ability to keep the dialogue open, enabling the student to explore the motives behind the disruption. As discussed in Chapter 2, disruptive behavior is caused by either tension-reduction or need-satisfaction. In both cases the student attempts to satisfy a need. Positive changes in behavior can occur only when the teacher and student get together and explore the nature of this need. Disruptive behavior creates a problem for the teacher; unmet needs create another problem for the disrupting student. The second step, then, to improving teacher–student dialogue is for the student, with the help of the teacher, to explore and clarify these unmet needs.

Although disclosing yourself to another is always a risk, my own experiences tell me it is a risk worth taking. The following quote given to me by Lee Rexroat, a friend and colleague, seems to say it best: "To risk is to be vulnerable. Being vulnerable is being always on the edge of pain, but not being vulnerable is not being fully alive."[4]

LISTENING SO STUDENTS WILL EXPLORE

Not all students with problems or unmet needs are disruptive. Cheryl, for example, who returns from recess and says to her teacher, "Tommy hit me!" obviously has a problem. So does George: A quiet, withdrawn senior, he responds to his English teacher's casual, "How are things going?" with "I can't get a date for the prom." Neither Cheryl nor George is disruptive, but they do own problems. Rather than having to confront these students, their teachers now need to respond as "helpers." This helping role, however, is often confusing and difficult to manage. Is George's English teacher expected to solve George's problem? If so, how does he go about it? If not, what other options are available?

George Gazda provides a model for helping teachers work with student-owned problems.[5] Generally, his approach is based on the belief that the best way to help others with problems is to respond in a way that enables them to find their own solutions. A "helper's" role does not entail solving other people's problems for them. Rather, it involves aiding them in the process of self-exploration— helping them examine, in detail, the nature of the concern and clarifying the various surface and underlying feelings involved. Self-exploration, in turn, leads to better self-understanding. As people explore the feelings and the nature of their problems, they can then develop new insights and a clearer view of the alternatives. Finally, such self-understanding makes it possible for the individual to act on these options. The helper's goal should be to respond in a way that facilitates this process.

Let's apply these ideas to disruptive behavior. Both the teacher and the student have problems. Consequently, teachers must first confront the student and let him or her know exactly what they are experiencing. After the confrontation, the teachers should then shift gears and enable students to share their concerns. This shift is often difficult to accomplish; we often respond in a way that is nonfacilitative. To demonstrate this tendency, let's go back to our example of Zelda and Mrs. Murphy. Mrs. Murphy confronts Zelda with a self-disclosing statement that describes her frustration and annoyance with Zelda's walking around the room and interfering with the day's lesson. If Zelda's behavior is the result of tension-reduction factors, she might respond to the confrontation with something like, "These stories are boring. I hate this reading class!" Five typical nonfacilitative teacher responses are:[6]

1. THE DETECTIVE: *What, specifically, is boring about them?* The Detective is probably the most popular of the nonfacilitative responses. It's not that there's anything inherently wrong with questions, but too often they focus merely on factual details. They usually control the flow of the dialogue and put the student on the defensive.

2. THE ANSWER MAN: *Zelda, you wouldn't be so bored if you buckled down and tried harder.* The Answer Man (or Answer Person, if you prefer) knows exactly what's right for the student. This type of teacher has the correct advice for any problem. Even though the advice may be beneficial, few students take it. (How often have you heard students like Zelda respond with, "You're right teacher. Thank you. I'll buckle down and try harder right now!") The Answer Man may occasionally play the Detective before giving the advice.

3. HOUDINI: *You're just imagining things, Zelda. This story is really quite interesting.* Houdini makes problems disappear by telling the student the problem doesn't exist. This illusion, however, is not long-lasting. Few people deny the validity of their own perceptions. It's not likely that Zelda would say, "You're right, teacher. I must be mistaken."

4. THE CANDY MAN: *Cheer up, Zelda. We'll have some really*

exciting stories next week. The Candy Man (Candy Person?) can't stand to talk about anything unpleasant. Consequently he or she gushes happy, sweet phrases in hopes of making these unpleasant feelings go away. The Candy Man becomes nervous and scared when confronted with gut feelings.

5. THE PSYCHIATRIST: *Zelda, you're being oversensitive. You're just a poorly motivated person.* The psychiatrist, good at analyzing and labeling problems, has an unlimited store of labels to be tacked on any problem. Unfortunately labeling a problem never solves it. (A poster hanging in my office sums up the psychiatrist's effectiveness: "Just because you're paranoid doesn't mean they're not out to get you.")

In addition to these five nonfacilitators, Generals and their non-disclosing buddies can also respond to student-owned problems. Their remarks would be equally devastating.

The process of helping based on self-exploration and self-understanding is not easy to bring about in the classroom. It requires time and skill of the teacher. If the teacher also owns a problem, as in the case of Mrs. Murphy, a mutual solution must be found. The following chapter details a seven-step approach, called "Behavior Negotiating," that can be used to find mutual solutions to teacher- and student-owned problems. The remainder of this chapter focuses on the difficulties and skills necessary to facilitate student self-exploration.

Time Out to Help

Time is the first prerequisite to helping. The teacher and student must have some time to get together and talk about their concerns. When dealing with problems, either student-owned, teacher-owned, or both, we must make time for interaction. We have no choice. If we can't find time to talk with students, then we're not going to solve problems.

A great deal of time is not required. Often, just fifteen minutes a day for teachers and students to interact alone is all that is needed. Given the compact schedules of today's schools, this time is not easy to find. Junior and senior high school teachers, especially, complain of not having time to talk with students. It amazes me that both teachers and students are in school about eight hours a day, and they can't find fifteen minutes to get together and talk.

Before or after school is not the answer. Not only is this time restricted by tight bus schedules, but it also bears the punitive connotation associated with "staying after school." While most teachers have prep periods to work with students, the odds are about seven or eight to one against a junior or senior high school student having a study hall during that time. Furthermore, some teachers become quite upset if another asks to talk with a student during their class. For example, I received a phone call from such a teacher when I was teaching in the junior high. I had given a student a pass to see me during my prep period, assuming that his teacher may choose to honor it or not. As I was sitting in the departmental office, I received a phone call from his teacher, who was furious. "Who do you think you are giving a student a pass to get out of my class," he shouted at me. Since it was obvious the teacher was having a problem, I did my best to understand his concern without becoming defensive. By the end of the conversation his anger had subsided, and he even offered to let the student out, if it was *really* important. I apologized for not checking with him first and said I would make other arrangements.

I know of one high school that has a fifteen-minute break each morning. What an excellent opportunity for teachers and students to get together and talk! Unfortunately, most of the faculty go to the lounge for a cup of coffee while the students slip outside for a cigarette. Maybe teachers need a fifteen-minute break from the students. I'm sure they want one from us. If that's the case, why not schedule another fifteen minutes for interaction. Evidently few teachers think this is important. If they did, they would fight to have it put into the master contract.

Using class time for this purpose is probably not a good idea, although it may be the only option available to some teachers. If so, then I suggest you arrange the class activities so that you can talk with the student in a place away from the others. The choice of whether to stop the class to deal with a problem immediately or to put it off to a more convenient time is a function of the severity of the problem. In Zelda's case, Mrs. Murphy might say something like, "I can see that you're upset by this, Zelda. If you can return to your seat, I'll be able to talk with you about it in ten minutes when the aide arrives." Each teacher establishes his or her own reputation for following through in situations like this. If Mrs. Murphy has a history of being lax or of forgetting to get back to students, Zelda may not take this option. On the other hand, if Zelda is sure that Mrs. Murphy will follow up, she will likely go along with the solution.

Developing Listening Skills

Certain listening skills help us avoid responding to students like the Detective or the Answer Man. If our goal is to help students explore their feelings and concerns, then we must convince the student that we care and that we are interested. Our purpose is to try to understand students, not to solve their problems or to change their perceptions.

Assume, for example, that you are Mrs. Murphy. After the aide arrives, you talk with Zelda about her boredom. You try to be understanding, but the conference doesn't seem to accomplish much. You feel frustrated and perplexed about what to do next. Just then the bell rings, and it's time for your lunch break. You take your brown bag, containing a peanut butter sandwich and an apple, and slowly walk to the faculty lounge. You're feeling depressed about your problem with Zelda, and the peanut butter sandwich doesn't seem very appealing. You get a cup of coffee and sink back into the overstuffed sofa donated by the PTA. As you're slipping off your shoes, Mrs. Perfectpitch, the music teacher, walks in eating a Big Mac. She sits down next to you and says, "What's the problem, Mary? You look like you just went ten rounds with Mohammed Ali." The rest of the conversation is as follows:

You: I don't know. I guess I'm just tired and maybe a little depressed.

Mrs. P: Why are you depressed?

You: I'm having a problem with one of my students. I can't seem to get anywhere with her.

Mrs. P: What's her name?

You: Zelda Jones.

Mrs. P: Really. What did she do?

You [You don't feel much like talking about it, but you answer.]: Oh, a lot of things. She's been walking around the room and disturbing the others. She even kicked over the wastebasket today.

Mrs. P: Oh, I remember Zelda. She's just overactive.

You: Yes, I guess she is.

Mrs. P: What you need to do, Mary, is have a talk with her, and let her know you won't tolerate that kind of behavior. You give a kid like that a centimeter, and she'll try to take a kilometer!

You: I guess you're right. But I've just talked with her, and it didn't seem to do any good.

Teacher–Student Dialogue

94

MRS. P: *Well, I have to go now. Cheer up, Mary. She can't be that bad.*

As Mrs. Perfectpitch leaves, you feel even more depressed. You take a bite from the peanut butter sandwich and put it back in the bag. You then close your eyes and wonder why you ever went into teaching. A few minutes later, Mr. Palette, the art teacher walks in. He gets a cup of the six-hour-old coffee, and takes a seat next to you.

MR. P: *Hi, Mary! You look tired.*

YOU: *Hi, Rex. I guess I am. I'm trying to work up enough courage to face the afternoon with my class.*

MR. P: *Evidently you're not looking forward to it."* [He replies in a friendly, mellow tone.]

YOU: *I'm not. I've been having a problem with Zelda Jones. She kicked over the wastebasket this morning.*

MR. P: *Sounds like she has been getting under your skin.*

YOU: *Yes, she was walking around the room and disturbing the others. When I said something to her, she told me the reading was boring and that she hated the class. I tried to talk with her when the aide arrived, but we didn't seem to get anywhere.*

MR. P: *It must be frustrating for you not being able to reach her.*

YOU: *It is! I let her know that I was angry with her behavior, but all she could say was the class was boring. I kept trying to tell her that she had to work at reading if she wanted to improve, but she didn't seem to listen. I have no idea how she's going to act this afternoon.*

MR. P: *She doesn't seem to share your concern about reading,*

Teacher–Student Dialogue

95

and you're afraid she may continue to disrupt the class. It sounds like you're feeling helpless about what to do with her.

YOU: I really am. I'm just not sure which way to turn. I thought of sending her down to the principal's office, but I doubt if that'll help. He's really part of the problem.

MR. P: I'm not sure I follow you, Mary.

YOU: Well, I know some of the things we do in reading are boring, but the reading tests are next week, and you know how important he thinks they are!

MR. P: Yes, he's a real fanatic for test scores. You seem worried that if your kids don't do well, he's going to blame you for it.

YOU: Yes, I guess that's part of the problem. With the decreasing enrollments, I'm afraid he may use the test scores to decide which teachers to lay off. [After a few moments of silence you continue.] The other thing that bothers me is I really want to be a good teacher. I want my students to learn how to read and to like it, in spite of the tests.

MR. P [Puts down his coffee and lights up a cigarette.]: You seem to be in a bind here, Mary. You're worried about keeping your job, but you also seem to be wondering if maybe you're not doing it right. It must be very discouraging for you.

YOU: It sure is Rex. I know Zelda is bored because of the way I'm teaching the class. I'm following the curriculum guide, word for word, hoping that will help the test scores. At the same time I want to say to hell with the damn curriculum guide and try some exciting things that will help the kids learn to like reading.

MR. P: You seem to know what you can do to solve the bore-

dom, but you're afraid the test scores will suffer if you do it?

You: *Yes, that's it. I guess I'm just afraid to teach the way I know how. I'm letting those darn tests turn me into a nagging, insensitive machine.*

You both sit there for awhile without saying anything. After a few moments the bell rings, ending your lunch period. You're feeling better now, although you're not sure why. You even decide to eat your apple on the way to class. As Rex gets up and pours out the remainder of his coffee, you look at him with a warm smile on your face. All you can say is, "Thanks."

Looking back at this little melodrama, both Mrs. Perfectpitch and Mr. Palette found themselves in helping roles. You were a fellow teacher experiencing a problem, and both wanted to help. Mrs. Perfectpitch, unfortunately, became a victim of the villains discussed in the first part of this chapter. She thought she would help by playing Detective, Psychiatrist, Answer Man, and Candy Man. Her intentions were honorable—her approach ineffective. Mr. Palette, on the other hand, avoided the nonfacilitators. He did not take it upon himself to solve your problem. Rather, he concentrated on being warm, accepting, and empathetic. There was nothing mystical or complicated in his approach. He simply tried to let you know he cared about you as a person and wanted to understand your feelings and concerns. If we could have observed the interaction, he probably would have looked at you more than Mrs. Perfectpitch did, and his tone of voice would probably have been more relaxed. He also showed more respect for you than did Mrs. Perfectpitch. He believed you to be a person of worth, capable of expressing yourself and of having the ability to solve your own problem. Since he had this respect, he did not need to give you cheap advice off the top of his head.

Empathy and Acceptance

Another major difference between these two teachers is that Mr. Palette was trying to respond to you empathetically. *Empathy* is not a complicated word reserved for therapists. It is simply letting another person know that you are trying to understand the feelings and concerns they are sharing. It's not enough, however, to just say you understand. As an empathic listener, you must respond in a way that *shows* the person with the problem that you are trying to understand his or her feelings. For Mr. Palette to respond with empathy, he had to listen intently to your concerns. He looked for both verbal and nonverbal cues that indicated what you were feeling. Finally, he tried to check out if what he was hearing and sensing was accurate by repeating to you, in his own words, what he understood you to be saying. His paraphrasing enabled you to examine in more detail what you were feeling and encouraged you to continue your self-exploration.

An important prerequisite to empathetic listening is *acceptance*. This is often difficult for teachers to demonstrate, since many assume that acceptance means agreement. This assumption is false. *Acceptance* means we take what a person says as being real for them—not for us. We don't have to feel the same way or believe the same things. Since agreement is not necessary for acceptance, there's no reason to deny another's feelings, to argue with them, or to change them.

Responding with empathy does not solve your students' problems. Nevertheless, it increases the likelihood that your students will further explore their feelings and concerns. Such self-exploration should lead to better self-understanding and more appropriate behavior.

While empathetic, facilitative listening and responding is a learned skill, it does require a certain attitude or philosophy toward teaching and students that some teachers may not possess. This philosophy seems to be based on the following assumptions:

1. You must want to hear about the student's concern and be willing to take the time to get involved. You have to genuinely want to be helpful.

2. You must be willing to accept students' feelings as being real for them, whatever they may be or however different they are from yours.

3. You must have a deep feeling of trust in students' capacity to handle their feelings, to work through them, and to find their own solutions.

4. Finally, you must be able to see students as persons separate from you—as separate individuals—with their own lives and own identities.

Only when you can agree with these four assumptions can you truly acquire the skills of empathetic listening.

Many educators are anxiously awaiting the day when someone will develop an approach for dealing with discipline problems that works for all teachers with all students. Given the diversity of teacher personalities and the complexity of student problems, that day is far in the future. Until then, each of us must continue the search for finding our own approaches that work best with most students. What follows is a method for dealing with discipline problems that has worked successfully for me and for many other teachers who have tried it. It will not work for all teachers, nor will it *solve* all problems. I offer it for your consideration.

Behavior Negotiating is a seven-step method for dealing with classroom discipline problems. It is derived from a synthesis of William Glasser's Reality Therapy, Thomas Gordon's Conflict Resolution, and Rudolph Dreikurs' Democratic Methods. If you look closely, you might even find a touch of Behavior Modification,

5

DEALING WITH
DISRUPTIVE BEHAVIOR

(how can I fix their wagons?)

which I hope is no more than a touch. Before plunging into the steps of Behavior Negotiating, it may be helpful to examine the approaches it attempts to synthesize.

WILLIAM GLASSER'S REALITY THERAPY

William Glasser advocates a technique for dealing with discipline called Reality Therapy.[1] His cookbook to success, while easy to memorize, is, for many teachers, much more difficult to put into practice. According to Glasserians, when teachers are faced with a little Johnnie whose behavior is not in accordance with accepted standards, they are advised to:

1. *get involved with the student, make friends with him, express concern for him as a person;*

2. *deal with his present behavior, avoid being a historian who talks about how many times the student transgressed in the past;*

3. *get the student to make a value judgment about what he is doing (is it helping him?);*

4. *assuming he has agreed that what he has been doing is not in his best interest, help him develop a plan to change his behavior;*

5. *get a commitment from the student to keep the plan, in writing or by a handshake;*

6. *if he fails to keep the plan, don't ask for or accept any excuses; and*

7. *don't punish the student for broken plans, but rather go back to step three and start over again.*

While Glasser has emphasized that this approach works only if certain assumptions regarding the classroom environment are met (that is, that kids find some value in the class and that they are involved in making the rules and have a clear understanding of them), some teachers continue to have difficulty using the technique. The breakdown usually takes the form of a series of broken plans and half-hearted commitments. Many students learn very quickly that the rules of the game have changed, and they have little difficulty in devising new strategies for winning. Plans can become superficial agreements: "I will not drop my books on the floor for the rest of the semester"—*Bang!*—"You didn't say I couldn't drop Billy's books!" They can also become broad, all-encompassing generalities: "I will be good forever"—*Bang!*—"I didn't know that meant I couldn't drop books!"

Glasser has repeatedly stated in his writing and in his talks throughout the country that his major concern is with the overt behavior of the student, rather than with feelings. In his clinical practice of Reality Therapy, when a client begins to talk about feelings, Glasser quickly shifts the direction of the dialogue to the client's overt behavior. The rationale for this shift seems to be based on his belief that once behavior is changed, a client's feelings also change. It appears, however, that this emphasis on behavior and behavior change by classroom teachers seems to be the reason for so many broken plans. When a disruption occurs, and the teacher and student get together to talk about it, all efforts are too often centered on producing a compact little plan to change behavior. Students quickly learn that if they can come up with almost anything that appears to be a plan, the teacher leaves them alone, at least for a while.

Glasser points out that plans are generally of little value unless there is involvement between teacher and student. Students must also make the value judgment that their present behavior is not in their best interest. Many teachers seem to overlook this point in their rush to produce plans. I find it impossible to envision a true, honest, involved relationship between a teacher and a student without an understanding and sharing of feelings. If I do not know or show an interest in a student's feelings, how can I expect us to be involved? Glasser has defined involvement as being personal and making friends with the student. If I had friends who did not show an interest in my feelings, I wouldn't consider them my friends for very long.

If the teacher truly expects to be involved and to facilitate a value change on the part of the student, considerable effort must be made to deal with that student's attitudes, feelings, and thoughts about behavior. Without the clarification and understanding of these attitudes, feelings, and thoughts, teachers cannot bring about the value change which, according to Glasser, is a prerequisite to producing a behavior change. Few students can make a meaningful and personal value change without exploring and clarifying their attitudes, feelings, and thoughts. Only when students internalize this value change—when the behavior problem becomes the student's rather than the teacher's—do they make a real commitment to behavior change.

So we come back again to the need for communication skills: The essence of Reality Therapy is involvement, and the essence of involvement is communication. Unfortunately, Reality Therapy does little to help teachers communicate more effectively with their students. At times we must confront students, and at times we must listen facilitatively. A humanistic approach for dealing with disruptive behavior must help teachers confront students without injuring the teacher–student relationship (involvement) or the self-esteem of the student. Furthermore, such an approach must help teachers develop skills of listening in order to facilitate student self-exploration and value clarification.

THOMAS GORDON'S
CONFLICT RESOLUTION

A second approach for dealing with disruptive behavior is Thomas Gordon's Conflict Resolution.[2] Conflict Resolution, or Method III as he sometimes calls it, originated from his attempts to help parents deal more effectively with their children. After experiencing some success with the method at this level, he began advocating the approach as a way for teachers to deal with their disruptive students.

Unlike Glasser's Reality Therapy, Conflict Resolution is based primarily on the skills of confronting and of facilitative listening. This "no-lose" method of resolving conflicts, according to Gordon, requires a step-by-step problem-solving process similar to John Dewey's "scientific method." The steps, as they apply to Conflict Resolution, are:

1. *Define the problem in terms of conflicting needs between the teacher and the student.*

2. *Generate possible solutions by brainstorming.*

3. *Evaluate the solutions in terms of meeting the needs of both the teacher and the student.*

4. *Make a decision that's mutually agreeable.*

5. *Determine how to implement the decision.*

6. *Assess the success of the solution after it has been implemented.*[3]

A primary strength of Gordon's method rests in its dedication to helping teachers communicate more honestly with their students. The first step of defining the problem in terms of conflicting needs, for example, requires that the teacher be trained in the skills of confronting and of listening. More than half of the content in Gordon's books are devoted to this purpose. A second advantage of the Gordon method is his clarification of problem ownership. He believes that disputes between teachers and students are often the results of conflicting needs. If, for example, two students are talking to each other while I'm trying to present a lesson, then I own a problem—I have a need for them to stop interfering. If this is the only chance they have to discuss their double date for Saturday night, then they also own a problem—they have a need to talk. Conflict Resolution is a method for resolving these conflicting needs.

A fundamental prerequisite to the Gordon approach is that the teachers agree to give up their use of power over the student. When using Conflict Resolution, according to Gordon, power becomes invisible and irrelevant. The teacher must refuse to use it. The student therefore needs no counterpower. Unfortunately, this is precisely the point at which many teachers balk at the use of Conflict Resolution in their classrooms. For them to give up power over their students is tantamount to an open invitation for chaos. "If I give up the little power that I have," a teacher in my class commented, "my classroom would make the monkey cage at the zoo look like a funeral procession!"

I see two reasons for this confusion over the role of power in Conflict Resolution. First, the approach Gordon advocates for teachers is almost identical to that developed for parents. It appears easier for parents to give up the use of power over a son or daughter than it is for teachers to give up power over their students. A parent is responsible only for the relationship with one child. Decisions affecting that child certainly have consequences for the entire family, but the family unit is small enough for all to have equal input. The teacher, on the other hand, is not only responsible for the student that precipitates the needs conflict, but for the entire class as well. I'm therefore not sure that an identical approach is possible in both the parents' and the teachers' situations.

A second, and probably more significant, reason for the confusion can be found in the distinction between the words "power" and "authority." Teachers, as a function of their role, are given authority over students; I don't believe Gordon is advocating that we give up that authority. To avoid chaos, we must have control within the classroom, and our authority allows—no, it demands—that we establish such control. Its purpose is to maintain a sense of order in the learning environment. Only when we convert authority into power, through the use of rewards and punishments, does Gordon protest, because power goes a step beyond maintaining control. It enforces the personal needs of the teacher, rather than the control demanded by the social order. When student needs are sacrificed to meet teacher demands, resentment and counterpower become the by-products. While implied, this distinction is not made clear by the Gordon approach. Consequently, many teachers are reluctant to use Conflict Resolution in their classrooms.

RUDOLF DREIKURS' DEMOCRATIC METHODS

A third approach for dealing with disruptive behavior is the methods and techniques advocated by Rudolf Dreikurs.[4] While not organized into a step-by-step procedure, Dreikurs' suggestions of "winning the child," using diagnostic questions, encouragement, and substituting logical consequences for punishment have been of great benefit to classroom teachers. In addition, he offers specific suggestions for dealing with students whose motives for disrupting are to satisfy the various personal needs discussed in Chapter 2.

Dreikurs' concept of "winning the child" is similar to Glasser's concept of involvement. If discipline is a process of helping students learn the value of obeying necessary rules and procedures, then teachers and students must become allies. Teachers, through their words and actions, must gain and maintain the child's confidence. First impressions are important: Many students are apprehensive when they meet a new teacher. To overcome these feelings, teachers must take a personal interest in the student. They can reassure students by being friendly and by showing interest in them as individuals. Dreikurs suggests that teachers take the time to become acquainted with the backgrounds, personality traits, or special interests of their students. There is no definite technique or simple secret for winning the child. Each teacher must find his or her own personal approach. What may work with one student may not work with another. Tone of voice, facial expressions, and physical proximity are just as important as words in this process. Good relationships between teachers and students cannot be taken for granted—they must be nourished.

Encouragement, logical consequences, and diagnostic questions are additional concepts advocated by Dreikurs. Each contributes to a step in Behavior Negotiating and is discussed in that context.

BEHAVIOR NEGOTIATING: A SYNTHESIS

What follows is a synthesis of the works of Glasser, Gordon, and Dreikurs into a seven-step approach for dealing with disruptive behavior. I call the approach Behavior Negotiating. It seems to work best when the following assumptions are met:

1. *We do whatever necessary to ensure that a minimum of 51*

percent of what students do in school is seen by them as being of value.

2. *Deficiencies in students' behavior in no way detract from their personal worth as human beings.*

3. *While teachers and students differ in experience, they are equal in their need for respect.*

4. *The teacher possesses the skills of listening facilitatively and of confronting without injuring the relationship with the student or the student's self-esteem.*

5. *The teacher and student have the time and place to discuss a problem alone.*

6. *Students are aware of the behaviors that are acceptable and unacceptable in the classroom.*

The first assumption deals with the value of school to the life of the student. It is based on the belief that Behavior Negotiating is most effective when students believe that *most* of what they do in school is of value to their lives. The assumption is optimistic. It doesn't demand that *everything* students do be of value. Such a demand would be impossible to meet. My experience has been that students do many things that they do not find of immediate value if they have the belief that *most* of what they do is of value.

This assumption holds true for teachers also. We do many things as teachers that are not rewarding or that we see as of little value: collecting milk money, determining grades, attending faculty meetings, and so on. If, however, we believe that most of what we do as teachers is rewarding to our lives, we perform these necessary but nonrewarding tasks. However, if the balance scale becomes reversed, we tend to reject teaching. If *most* of what we do as teachers is not of value to us personally, then we seriously consider a different profession. Students operate in the same way. If *most* of what they are doing in school is perceived as not being of value to their lives, they then reject the whole package.

The second assumption, which suggests we differentiate between what persons do and what they are, and the third assumption, which proposes that teachers and students are equal in their entitlement to respect, constitute the underlying philosophy of humanistic teaching. Differentiating between one's behavior and one's humanity is often not easy to do. A common tendency is to reject persons when we reject their behavior. Humanistic teaching, however, demands that we separate the two. We may become angry and upset by some students' behavior, but we must avoid giving up on them as persons. Likewise, we as teachers are not entitled to more respect than we give our students. While we may differ in experience, we are equal in our humanity. This equality makes it impossible for us as humanistic teachers to demand more respect than we are willing to give.

The fourth assumption requires that teachers possess the skills of listening and confronting, as discussed previously. While I believe these skills can be learned and integrated, some people have difficulty in doing so. Their communication patterns are so entrenched that they are either unable or unwilling to give them up. Maybe the ability to integrate these skills is directly related to the teacher's commitment to assumptions 2 and 3.

The fifth assumption requires that the teacher and student have a time and place to interact. A great deal of time is not necessary—fifteen minutes a day may be all that is needed. Nevertheless, if *some* time is not available, then teachers have little choice but to rely on fear or rewards as their only control.

The last assumption of Behavior Negotiating requires that students be aware of the differences between acceptable and unacceptable behavior in the classroom. Rules and procedures are necessary if classrooms are to function without chaos, and presumably the teacher and students have discussed the nature and reasons for such limits. The discussion might have resulted in a list of rules acceptable to both the teacher and the students, as Glasser suggests, or it might have been a more informal agreement on acceptable and unacceptable behavior. I prefer the second approach, as most lists of classroom rules are either too specific or too broad to be of much value.

STEPS TO BEHAVIOR NEGOTIATING

STEP 1: When you have a problem with students' behavior, let them know how the behavior affects your feelings and needs.

Steps I and II of Behavior Negotiating are based on the confronting and listening skills presented in the previous chapter. Specifically, when students disrupt the learning environment, their behavior creates a problem for the teacher; disruptive behavior generates feelings within the teacher. Confrontation becomes necessary, and the nature of the confrontation sets the tone for resolving the problem. This first step requires teachers to be open to these feelings and to be willing to share them with the student. In addition, disruptive behavior also generates consequences. These consequences usually interfere with the learning environment and the teachers' need to meet instructional objectives.

When dealing with a disruptive incident, then, it is suggested that the teacher confront the student by defining the unacceptable behavior nonjudgmentally, share the feelings created by the behavior, and express the consequences of the behavior as they relate to the teacher's needs. Such nonjudgmental confrontations avoid injuring the self-esteem of the student. They also foster a continued dialogue between the teacher and the student, maximizing the likelihood of finding a solution to the problem.

The following six problem situations demonstrate the seven steps of Behavior Negotiating. Assume that you are a seventh-grade math teacher, and the following situations occur during one of your classes.

EXAMPLE 1
Suzie and Terry are both good students and leaders in their class. They are friends, but they also seem to be in competition with each other. As you begin the class, you notice Suzie trying to poke Terry with a pencil.

EXAMPLE 2
Johnnie is a student who shows little interest in math. He does D and F work and is constantly disrupting the class by his attention-seeking antics. You have sent him to the principal's office twice within the last month, but his behavior has not changed. As you are explaining today's assignment, you notice that he is walking around the room and talking with some of his friends.

EXAMPLE 3
Mary is a quiet, withdrawn girl who does A work. As you are explaining the assignment, she is clicking her pen repeatedly, and it is annoying you.

EXAMPLE 4
Tom does average work in class and does not cause any problems. He has, however, been late for class three times during the past week. Today he walks in five minutes after the class has started. You have already turned in your attendance card.

EXAMPLE 5

Bill is a conscientious, hard-working student in your class. After you have explained the day's lesson and have given students time to start working on tomorrow's assignment, Bill gets out of his seat and walks over to talk with one of his friends.

EXAMPLE 6

Don is an angry, withdrawn student who does just enough work to earn a D-minus. He radiates contempt and resentment toward you and anyone else associated with the school. As the class begins its homework assignment, you observe him sitting on the top of his desk staring out the window.

The following are ways to confront these students, using step I of Behavior Negotiating:

EXAMPLE 1

"Suzie, when you poke that pencil at Terry, I'm afraid someone's going to be hurt!"

EXAMPLE 2

"Johnnie, I find it frustrating when you walk around the room and talk with the other students, because I can't complete today's lesson."

EXAMPLE 3

"Mary, when you keep clicking that pen, I can't concentrate on what I'm doing."

EXAMPLE 4

"Tom, I am annoyed when you come late to class because I have to change the attendance card, and it interferes with our getting started on time."

EXAMPLE 5

"Bill, I don't understand why you are out of your seat."

EXAMPLE 6

"Don, I'm afraid that desk may fall over when you sit on the top of it like that."

The wording in these examples may seem artificial to many readers. Each teacher must use the words that are most natural to him or her. The words used are not nearly as important as the message conveyed. Refer to the section on confrontation skills (pp. 79–88) for a more detailed discussion. The observant reader will note that some of the confrontations do not include all three parts of Gordon's "I-message." In four of the examples, the teacher is expressing feelings of anger, fear, frustration, and annoyance. In example 3, the teacher describes the behavior and its effects but does not mention the mild irritation she may be experiencing. This seems to be implied by the teacher's inability to concentrate. In example 5, the teacher is merely experiencing uncertainty. It's important that such confrontations be appropriate to the teacher's internal experiences.

Step II: Try to understand the students' feelings, thoughts, and needs.

The second step of Behavior Negotiating requires that teachers allow or enable students to share their feelings, thoughts, and opinions about the behavior. Students may also have needs that are being frustrated, so teachers must listen and accept these feelings and thoughts as being real for the student. Listening and accepting do not mean agreeing. They simply imply that we try to understand students' perceptions of their environment. It is important that we do not allow this step to turn into an argument. Our purpose at this point is to understand the student—not to defend, deny, or change the student's perceptions.

As a result of prior experiences with teachers, some students may be reluctant to share their feelings and thoughts with the teacher. Sometimes we can overcome this tendency by avoiding value judgments and by paraphrasing the student's feelings and thoughts. As pointed out in a more detailed discussion of this skill in Chapter 4, the purpose of such paraphrasing is to test our perception of the student's concern. We want to let students know that we are trying to understand their feelings, needs, and views of the situation.

Let's look at some cases of facilitating students' feelings, thoughts, and needs:

EXAMPLE 1

SUZIE: *Well, she started it!*

TEACHER: *Terry did something to make you angry?*

SUZIE: *Yeah, she poked me with her pencil.*

TEACHER: *And now you would like to get even by poking her.*

SUZIE: *Yup, I would.*

TEACHER: *You both seem to be pretty angry with each other. The three of us are going to have to get together and work this out. We can wait until lunch, or I can get the vice-principal to continue with the class while we talk now.*

SUZIE: *I don't care; Terry started it.*

TEACHER [to Terry]: *What do you think, Terry?*

TERRY: *Well, we better do it now or the crybaby is going to be on me all hour!*

TEACHER: *I'll call Mr. W on the intercom.* [Mr. W. is busy and can't take the class.] *We'll have to wait until lunch to take care of this, girls. Can you put off the battle until class is finished, or would one of you like to move your seat?*

SUZIE: *I'd be happy to move away from that s.o.b.!"*

TEACHER: *That language bothers me, Suzie. I can't allow it in here. Can you sit over here until we can discuss this further?*

SUZIE: *Yeah.*

EXAMPLE 2
JOHNNIE: *Well, it's boring just sitting there and doing all those problems.*

TEACHER: *You don't see much value in doing the assignment?*

JOHNNIE: *Yeah, it's for the birds.*

TEACHER: *You would rather not have to do your work and be able to just walk around?*

JOHNNIE: *Yeah, anything to relieve this boredom.*

TEACHER: *You seem pretty frustrated by this class, Johnnie. I'd like to get together with you during lunch today and talk about this some more. Can you return to your seat and wait until then?*

JOHNNIE: *Sure.*

EXAMPLE 3
MARY: *I'm sorry, I didn't realize I was doing it. I'll stop.*

TEACHER: *Thank you.*

EXAMPLE 4
TOM: *Well, I have gym class before this, and he never gives us enough time to shower.*

TEACHER: *You don't have enough time to get cleaned up after gym?*

TOM: *Yeah, I try to hurry, but I just don't seem to be able to make it.*

TEACHER: *You don't want to be late, but there seems to be little you can do about it.*

TOM: *Yeah, I really try!*

TEACHER: *Let's get together during fourth hour and see if we can solve it.*

TOM: *Okay.*

EXAMPLE 5

BILL: *I forgot my pencil, and I was asking Chuck if I could borrow one of his. He doesn't have an extra one, though.*

TEACHER: *You just want to borrow a pencil?*

BILL: *Yeah.*

TEACHER: *You may use mine until the end of class.*

BILL: *Thank you, I'll give it back as soon as the bell rings.* [He returns to his seat and begins the assignment.]

EXAMPLE 6

Don ignores the teacher's comments. He continues to sit on top of the desk and stare out the window. He acts as if the teacher is not even there.

TEACHER [In a low voice]: *You seem upset about something, Don. Can you tell me about it?* [Don continues to ignore the teacher.]

It is important to emphasize that if the student appears more emotionally upset than the teacher, *steps I and II should be reversed.* The reason for this reversal is to allow the individual with the strongest emotions to vent these feelings *before* he or she can be expected to listen to the concerns of another. In examples 1 and 6, it probably would have been more beneficial for the teacher to start the dialogue by asking the student what was happening. After facilitating a clarification of the student's perceptions, the teacher would then disclose his or her feelings and concerns about the situation.

For some classroom disruptions, steps I and II are enough to terminate the problem. Often, students are unaware that their behavior is creating a problem for the teacher and the nonjudgmental confrontation of step I might be all that is needed. Mary, in example 3, demonstrates this. Likewise, the teacher might be unaware of students' perceptions about their environment, and step II might result in a small change to resolve the problem. The teacher, giving Bill a pencil in example 5, demonstrates this. Some students may respond to confrontation with a shrug of the shoulders or even by completely ignoring the teacher, as does Don in example 6. Suzie, Johnnie, and Tom, on the other hand, are willing to share their perceptions.

At some point in the Behavior Negotiating process, the teacher must decide whether to continue the dialogue during the class period or to postpone it until the teacher and student can have time to discuss it alone. This is never an easy decision. It is determined, in part, by the severity of the problem, the teacher and student's disposition, and the time factors involved. In the examples we are using, Johnnie and Tom are both willing to postpone further discussion. In such cases it is crucial that teachers establish a reputation of always following through on these matters. If they schedule a time to continue the dialogue and then have a tendency not to follow through, they decrease the likelihood of students' accepting this option. In example 1, the teacher has decided that Suzie and Terry's problem is important enough to ask the vice-principal to take the class while the teacher deals with it. In some schools this may be unrealistic. It's been my experience, however, that many administrators would rather take your class for ten minutes than have to deal with the problem. In any event, the teacher should work this out with the administrator before he or she calls.

STEP III: *Help the students examine the* motive *for their behavior*

As discussed in Chapter 2, disruptive behavior is goal oriented. Its purposes are to reduce tension caused by the immediate environment, satisfy personal needs, or both. At this point in Behavior Negotiating the teacher tries to help the student acknowledge these motives. A relationship based on mutual trust and honesty increases the likelihood that such an acknowledgment will take place. The student may well turn mute if such a relationship has not been fostered. To encourage this reflection, we must avoid making value judgments about the student. Students are neither good nor bad because they have a strong need for attention. There are simply acceptable or unacceptable ways for them to meet that need in the classroom. Avoiding such value judgments increases the chances for an honest evaluation from the student.

If students have difficulty acknowledging their motives (often the case when dealing with the goals of attention, power, revenge, or noninvolvement), we might be able to help them with diagnostic questioning. Diagnostic questions are based on the teacher's hypothesis about the student's motive. The following are examples of some diagnostic questions:[5]

ATTENTION

1. *Could it be that you want me or the others in class to notice you?*

2. *Could it be that you want me to do something special for you?*

POWER

1. *Could it be that you want to show me that you can do what you want and that no one can stop you?*

2. *Could it be that you want to be the boss?*

REVENGE

1. *Could it be that you want to get even?*

2. *Could it be that you want to hurt me or the others in the class?*

NONINVOLVEMENT

1. *Could it be that you want to be left alone?*

2. *Could it be that you feel stupid and don't want others to know?*

Diagnostic questions provide the teacher with an opportunity to test out an impression about a student's goal. Acknowledging these goals is often threatening to students. Consequently, they might answer by saying no to the inquiry. With this in mind, Dreikurs suggests that the teacher be alert for a "recognition reflex" or nonverbal clues, such as a smile or glint in the eye that may indicate that the teacher is on target.

Suggesting a goal in the form of a diagnostic question, even though it may be verbally denied by the student, can still have an impact on behavior. The effect is similar to finding a fly in your coffee: After removing the insect, you can still drink the coffee, but it somehow never tastes the same. Attention-seekers who know that the teacher knows their real goal might continue to seek attention by their antics, but somehow their behavior is not as satisfying.

When dealing with tension-reduction disruptions, students will be more likely to acknowledge their motives. The frustration, anxiety, or boredom they may be experiencing usually comes out loud and clear.

Helping students examine their motives for disrupting will not, in itself, solve problems. However, it will make it possible for the teacher and student to explore ways to reduce the classroom-caused tensions. It will also make it possible to examine alternative ways for students to satisfy their personal needs.

Continuing with the examples we have been using, the following are illustrations of helping students examine the motives for their behavior.

EXAMPLE 1

TEACHER [to Suzie during lunch]: *Okay, as I see this, Terry poked you first and then you wanted to get even with her by poking her back.*

SUZIE: *Yeah, I want to teach her that she can't get away with poking me.*

EXAMPLE 2

TEACHER [to Johnnie during lunch]: *As I understand it, Johnnie, you find the work we're doing in class boring and you would rather walk around the room and talk with your friends.*

JOHNNIE: *That's right. I don't need to know how to solve equations. It has no value to me.*

TEACHER: *I see your frustration, Johnnie. Could it also be that you want a little attention from me or from the others in class?*

JOHNNIE: *I don't know.* [Teacher is silent.] *I guess so. It gets so boring just doing assignments. I like talking to my friends.*

TEACHER: *You wish you had more time to be with them rather than do your math.*

JOHNNIE: *Yeah.*

EXAMPLE 4

TEACHER [to Tom during prep period]: *Tom, as I understand it, you're coming late to my class because you don't have enough time to get showered after gym class. Is there something about my class that makes you want to be late?*

TOM: *No, that's not it at all. I really like coming here. It's just that I need more time to get showered after gym class.*

EXAMPLE 6

TEACHER [to Don as others are working on assignment]: *You evidently don't have much to say to me, Don. Could it be that you're trying to show me that I can't* make *you get off your desk?* [Don raises his eyebrows and shrugs his shoulders. He still does not say anything to the teacher.]

In example 1 it appears that Suzie's motive is to get even with Terry. She wants revenge for what Terry did to her. The teacher is a "third party" in this dispute. Often two students will agree to disagree for the attention they both receive from the disturbance. With Suzie and Terry, however, the conflict appears real. In example 2, Johnnie's behavior appears to be motivated by both tension-reduction and need-satisfaction. He seems bored and frustrated by the work in class, and also has a need for attention from his peers. The teacher's diagnostic question has helped him reflect on this need. Tom's goal in example 4 is to get to class on time. Nevertheless, something in the school environment is preventing him from doing so. Don, in example 6, may want to demonstrate that the teacher is powerless over him. His raised eyebrows and shrug of the shoulders appear to be a recognition reflex and might indicate that there is validity in the teacher's assumption about his motive. In any event, further exploration of his motive will not be possible until he and the teacher are able to establish more communication in their relationship.

STEP IV: *Help the students evaluate the results of their behavior.*

The purpose of this step is to encourage the students to evaluate their behavior and assume responsibility for it. The teacher has already made the value judgment that the behavior is unacceptable and cannot continue. Now it's up to the students to make an evaluation. To this end, the students are helped to examine the results of the behavior on themselves, the teacher, and others in the class. It is important that the value judgment focus on the *effects* or *results* of the behavior rather than the motive behind the behavior. The issue is not whether it is "right" or "wrong" to want attention, power, or revenge or to want to relieve frustration, boredom, or excitement. Rather, our purpose is to help students evaluate the effects of their behavior and the consequences that may have to be imposed when they hit others, walk around the room, shout out, or kick the wastebasket.

Some students may not agree with the teacher that their behavior is unacceptable. They may not see anything wrong with shouting out when they feel the urge. If such differences exist, it is important not to turn the dialogue into an argument. Discussion should center on the effects of the behavior on the student, teacher, and others in the class. Certain rules and procedures are necessary so that classrooms function without chaos. When these rules and procedures are not followed, certain logical consequences must be imposed. We cannot allow some students to meet their needs at the expense of ourselves or others in the class. It is assumed, of course, that these rules and procedures have been discussed with the class and that most students understand and agree with the necessity for having them.

The success or failure of the entire negotiating process often rests with this step. If our goal is to help students assume responsibility for their own behavior, then we must help them explore and evaluate the consequences of this behavior. While a particular student may not see anything wrong with shouting out whenever he or she feels like it, that student will probably agree that the consequences (isolation or removal from class) are not in his or her best interest. If the student fails to make this value judgment, then the teacher has little choice but to bypass the next step of behavior negotiating and move directly to step VI, enforcing logical consequences, until such time that a value judgment can be made.

I believe it important that we not use logical consequences as a *threat* to make students change. Imposing a logical consequence is not something *we* do to students but is something that students do to themselves as a result of their behavior. It is also important that we do everything possible to help students meet their needs within the classroom. We cannot allow these needs to be met at the expense of ourselves or other students, but we must be willing to explore alternatives that provide mutual satisfaction.

The following are examples of the teacher helping Suzie, Johnnie, Tom and Don evaluate the results of their behavior:

EXAMPLE 1
TEACHER [to Suzie]: *Do you think that poking her back is going to solve our problem, Suzie?*

SUZIE: *Yeah, it will teach her not to poke me.*

TEACHER: *Maybe it will, but I still have a problem because I can't allow you to fight in class. It's disturbing others and I'm afraid someone is going to get hurt.*

SUZIE: *Well, why didn't you say that to her when she poked me?*

TEACHER: *I didn't see Terry poke you, Suzie. It sounds as though you think I'm being unfair to you.*

SUZIE: *Yeah, I know you don't want us to fight in class, but she did poke me first, and I couldn't just let her get away with it.*

TEACHER: *I understand that you were upset and wanted to get even with her, Suzie, though I'm not sure that poking her back with your pencil was the best solution.* [To Terry] *Terry, how do you see this?*

TERRY: *I wasn't trying to hurt her. Besides, she's making a criminal case out of this. I was only teasing her.*

SUZIE: *Well, I don't like to be teased!*

TERRY: *I can see that!*

EXAMPLE 2

TEACHER [to Johnnie]: *It seems as though there are two problems here, Johnnie. You don't want to do your math because you don't find any value in it, and you like the attention you get from your friends when you walk around the room.*

JOHNNIE: *Yeah, that sums it up pretty good.*

TEACHER: *I can understand your boredom with math, Johnnie, and I think there are some ways I can help you find more value in it. I cannot, however, allow you to walk around the room when you feel like it.*

JOHNNIE: *What are you going to do to me?*

TEACHER: *I don't want to do anything to you Johnnie, except help you find some value in math.*

JOHNNIE: *Well that is a lost cause. I just don't like math. I never was very good at it. And besides, all that stuff on dividing fractions really has me confused. I tried to stay with it at the beginning but you got so far ahead of me that I could never get it.*

TEACHER: *You think I'm going too fast for you?*

JOHNNIE: *Just look at my tests! I got F's on the last two.*

TEACHER: *I thought it was because you weren't paying attention.*

JOHNNIE: *How can I pay attention to something I don't understand? As soon as you start explaining those problems on the board, I'm lost. I guess that's when I start walking around and talk with the other guys.*

TEACHER: *It sounds as if you could understand this stuff a little better you wouldn't need to walk around the room so much.*

JOHNNIE: *Yeah, but I'm so confused I'll never be able to understand it. Besides, I like talking to my friends, too.*

TEACHER: *I think I can find a way to help you work through all that confusion with fractions, Johnnie, but I'm not sure what we can do about your wanting attention from your friends.*

JOHNNIE: *Why don't you just let me talk to my friends whenever I feel like it?*

TEACHER: *No way, that's what you are doing now and it's driving me up a wall! I can't let that continue.*

JOHNNIE [smiles]: *I guess you are right. Maybe there is a way I can talk with them without bothering you.*

EXAMPLE 4

TEACHER [to Tom]: *You seem to be in a bind here, Tom. You don't want to be late, but you can't seem to help it.*

TOM: *Yeah, I know being on time for class is important to you, but the gym teacher requires that everyone take a shower before they can leave for their next class.*

EXAMPLE 6

TEACHER [to Don, quietly as others are working]: *It looks as though something important is bothering you, Don, and that you don't want to be in this class today. I'd like to help you with it, if you will let me.* [Don continues to sit on the top of his desk and ignore the teacher.]

In example 1, Suzie knew that she was not supposed to fight in class. She also felt victimized by Terry and believed her only recourse was to poke back. The teacher, however, is not concerned with putting blame on either student. The goal is to help the girls resolve their present conflict and to help Suzie explore alternatives to fighting in the classroom, even when it seems justified. The teacher will also want to discuss Terry's teasing behavior, but it may be more effective to treat this as a separate problem.

As indicated by the dialogue in example 2, Johnnie's behavior is the product of his frustration with math, as well as his need for attention from his friends. While the problems are closely related, they require separate value judgments and solutions. At first Johnnie complained that he was bored with math, although further exploration revealed that the boredom stemmed from his frustration and confusion with fractions. There may be several things that the teacher can do to help relieve this frustration. His attention-seeking behavior, however, is a separate problem.

Tom, in example 4, knows that his behavior is creating a problem for the teacher, but he is having difficulty finding a way to rectify the situation. Don, in example 6, continues to refuse to discuss the problem. He is unwilling to evaluate his behavior.

STEP V: Help the students explore and select a mutually agreed alternative to the disruptive behavior.

The purpose of this step is to help students find alternative ways of meeting their needs which do not disrupt the class. This step assumes, of course, that the teacher and student are in agreement that the student's behavior is inappropriate. If such a meeting of the minds has not been reached, then this step must be postponed.

The plan for alternative behavior has a higher chance for success if the student suggests it rather than the teacher. In any event, the plan must be clearly understood and acceptable to both parties. Once a plan that is mutually satisfying is established, Glasser suggests that the teacher seek from the student a commitment to keep it. He believes that a handshake or a written contract is necessary. I have found that a verbal agreement is often enough. It seems that the plan itself is not nearly as important as the relationship that develops between the teacher and student in the process of finding one.

The following examples show the process of exploring and selecting mutually agreed alternatives.

EXAMPLE 1

TEACHER [to Suzie and Terry]: *Well girls, what are we going to do about this?*

SUZIE: *Well, if you tell Terry to stop teasing me, I won't poke her either.*

TEACHER: *Terry?*

TERRY: *Well, it's no big thing.* [Silence.] *I didn't mean anything by it.*

SUZIE: *Fine, then let's just forget it.*

TERRY: *Sounds good to me.*

TEACHER: *Me too. Let's get some lunch.*

EXAMPLE 2

TEACHER [to Johnnie]: *You think that if you had some opportunities to work and talk with your friends in class, you wouldn't have to get out of your seat and walk around so much?*

JOHNNIE: *Yeah, maybe if we had more group discussions or if we could work with partners like we did in our first unit, it would be better.*

TEACHER: *I was planning some partner work for the next unit. Sounds like you think that will help.*

JOHNNIE: *Yeah, maybe Caesar and I could work on a project or something together. Then we could do our work for a while and talk for a while.*

TEACHER: *I guess I'm a little worried that you and Caesar will end up doing more talking than working.*

JOHNNIE: *Well, I can't guarantee that we won't, but why don't you let us try it. Maybe we'll surprise you.*

TEACHER: *Okay, fair enough. The three of us can get together tomorrow and we'll see what we can come up with.* [Pause] *I'd like to go back to that confusion you're having with fractions, Johnnie. I think there are some things that I can do to help you. Would you like to give it a try?*

JOHNNIE: Boy, I don't know. I'm so far behind that I don't think I'll ever catch up.

TEACHER: You sound pretty discouraged.

JOHNNIE: Yeah, I guess I am. My dad says I wasn't around the day that the good Lord handed out brains. Maybe he's right.

TEACHER: Oh yes, I remember that day very clearly. And I know you were there because you were sitting three seats away from me. As I recall, after the brains were handed out you got out of your seat and started to talk with Caesar. [Johnnie breaks out with a big grin.]

JOHNNIE: I'll have to tell that to my Dad the next time he says that to me. Boy, will he be surprised! [Pause] Do you think you really can help me learn fractions?

TEACHER: Yes, I'm certain of it, Johnnie. But it's going to take some time and effort on your part.

JOHNNIE: Well, on Tuesdays and Thursdays I have to wait thirty minutes after school for my bus. Can we use that time?

TEACHER: I have meetings on some of those afternoons, but I'm sure we can work around them. When do you want to get started?

JOHNNIE: How about tomorrow after school?

TEACHER: That's fine. I'll see you then.

EXAMPLE 4

TEACHER [To Tom]: What do you think we can do about it?

TOM: I don't know. Maybe I could just cut gym class.

TEACHER: Sounds like you dislike going there.

TOM: *Yeah, I really do. They herd us all together in those showers like cattle. I don't like that.*

TEACHER: *You dislike taking showers with the others?*

TOM: *Yeah, I guess that's why I'm always late. I try to hang around until the others finish before I go into the shower room. [Silence.] Sometimes I can get to the showers first, before the others get there. When I do that, I'm never late for class. I can't do it all the time, though, because sometimes I have to wait around and collect the equipment for our team.*

TEACHER: *I see your problem here, Tom. Have you explained it to Mr. J, the PE teacher?*

TOM: *I told him that I don't like collecting the equipment, but he says everyone has to take his turn. [Silence.] I guess I'm a little afraid to tell him why, though. I don't think he would understand. Would you explain the situation to him?*

TEACHER: *It sounds like you would like to tell Mr. J the real reason you don't like to collect the equipment, but it's a little scary for you. Are you certain you would want me to do it for you?*

TOM: *I don't really know for sure. I thought it would be easier for me if you did it. I'm just afraid that he will laugh at me.*

TEACHER: *You would find that pretty embarrassing?*

TOM: *Yeah, I sure would. He's just not very understanding of things like this. [Silence.] I think it would be better if I'm honest with him though.*

TEACHER: *I'd be happy to go with you, if you think it would help.*

TOM: *That sure would make it easier.*

TEACHER: *Would you like me to call him now and set up a meeting for the three of us.*

TOM: *Yeah, the sooner the better.*

EXAMPLE 6

TEACHER [To Don]: *Well, Don, what are we going to do about this?*

[Don ignores the teacher and continues to sit on top of his desk.]

Suzie and Terry's plan is simply to stop the teasing and poking. Such seemingly bitter flare-ups among students are often short-lived. The teacher's moralizing or preaching about appropriate behavior would serve no purpose at this point. Both girls know what's going on and are willing to stop. Nevertheless, the teacher may want to discuss three additional problems individually with Suzie and Terry. First, the teacher might want to help Suzie consider alternatives to fighting back when she is provoked by another's teasing. This could be done in a nonthreatening discussion with Suzie, or it could be part of a class discussion of fighting. A second issue is Suzie's inappropriate language in the class. The teacher has already expressed her feelings about it, and if it was just a spontaneous one-time occurrence, the teacher may decide to drop it at this point. However, if Suzie continues these outbursts, the teacher may want to use Behavior Negotiating with the problem. A third concern is Terry's teasing behavior. The teacher has not yet discussed this with Terry and may want to do so at a later time.

Johnnie's plan to work with Caesar on a project elicits some doubt from the teacher. Her decision to go along with it, however, shows a sense of trust in the two students and a willingness to give them a chance. Johnnie's second plan, to seek extra help with fractions, should be effective in reducing some of the frustration he is experiencing in the class.

Tom's problem seems more complicated than just coming late for class. His insecurity in the shower room requires some understanding from the PE teacher. Now that the problem is in the open, however, a reasonable solution should be easy to find.

The teacher is premature in searching for a plan for alternative behavior with Don. Don seems to be pushing for a power struggle. The teacher must be careful not to escalate the conflict.

STEP VI: *Apply logical consequences when necessary.*

When students are unwilling to share their perceptions, examine their motives, or agree to exploring alternative behaviors, then it may be necessary to enforce the most logical consequence to the unacceptable behavior until a dialogue can be resumed and an alternative behavior found. Simply stated, a *logical consequence* is an attempt to arrange the results of unacceptable behavior as closely as possible to the behavior itself. If, for example, a student spills paints during art class, the logical consequence is that he or she cleans them up. Unlike punishment, a logical consequence is logically related as closely as possible to the unacceptable behavior. If we decide to give a detention to the student who spills paints or force him or her to write a hundred times, "I will be more careful during art class," we are using punishment rather than logical consequences.

While punishment might occasionally stop the undesirable behavior, it can also produce other reactions. I can best explain this by using myself as an example. I probably have more atrocious handwriting than anyone I know. Indeed, it's a rare occasion in my classes when I pick up a piece of chalk and write something on the chalkboard. Not only is the chicken-scratch illegible, I detest doing it. I believe my handwriting is so grotesque because I spent my entire fifth grade learning to hate writing. It was my fifth-grade teacher who taught me to hate writing. She established the policy that whenever we would get out of line, talk out of turn, throw paper airplanes, or commit any of a hundred other transgressions, we would have to make a commitment that we would never do so again. The commitment took the form of a written statement—something like, "I'll never throw paper airplanes in this class again." To make sure that our devious little minds would not forget the importance of the commitment, she had us write the statement one hundred times. If we were absentminded enough to forget after that, she doubled the number of times for each additional offense.

I don't recall how many thousands of sentences I wrote that year, but it seemed that every free moment was devoted to the task. I became so proficient that I could hold three pencils in my hand at one time and make it look like each sentence was written independently. This accomplishment won me the admiration of the others in the class because when they tried it, the teacher could always tell that they had used more than one pencil, and she would make them start over again. Unfortunately, since fifth grade, I have never had the opportunity to use this finely developed skill of three-pencil writing. In fact, I now find it very difficult writing with one pencil. I'm not sure if her punishment by writing taught me to stop throwing airplanes or to raise my hand before I talked, but I know one thing—it taught me to hate writing. Even though I was good with three pencils, I loathed the task. Whenever I was assigned 200 sentences for this or 400 sentences for that, I cringed inside. I learned to hate pencils, paper, and anything else that had to do with writing.

Logical consequences can help teachers avoid the twofold danger of defeating their own purposes and causing unfortunate side effects in their students. In this sense, they are "safer" as well as more effective. In regard to classroom disruptions, exclusion seems to be the most widely used logical consequence. The exclusion should, however, related to the specific activity with which the student is having difficulty. If Frank, for example, is fighting on the playground, the logical consequence is that he can't be on the playground. There's no reason to exclude him from gym class or art class because of his playground behavior.

With some behaviors the distinction between logical consequences and punishment is not always clear. Is it punishment or logical consequence if the teacher decides to keep Mary in for recess because she didn't do her math problems? Further examining the characteristics of logical consequences and punishment will help answer that question.

CHARACTERISTICS OF LOGICAL CONSEQUENCES:

1. *When using logical consequences, the tone of voice is usually unemotional. A simple, matter-of-fact statement is made in a calm, friendly manner.*

2. *The consequence imposed is dependent on and logically related to the unacceptable behavior. The relationship is direct and easily discernible.*

3. *Judgments of individual goodness or badness are absent when using logical consequences. Focus is on the unacceptable behavior and its relationship to the consequence.*

4. *Logical consequences are designed to enable students to assume the responsibility to change their behavior.*

5. *Logical consequences express the reality of the situation.*

CHARACTERISTICS OF PUNISHMENT:

1. *The authority usually shows anger or resentment—either open or concealed—toward the student.*

2. The punishment rarely is directly or logically related to the unacceptable behavior.

3. Punishment has moralistic overtones. Unacceptable behavior is equated with badness.

4. The authority assumes the responsibility to change the student's behavior.

5. Punishment expresses the personal power of the authority.

Keeping Mary in for recess to do her math may be a punishment or logical consequence depending on the teacher's attitude. If the teacher uses this as a chance to show his power over Mary and moralizes about her lazy behavior, Mary begins to see it as punishment. On the other hand, it is a logical consequence if the teacher tries to show Mary in a friendly, nonjudgmental way, that the consequence for not doing her math during the allocated time is that she must use her recess time to finish it. Mary may still perceive this as a form of punishment. It is important, therefore, that the teacher focus on the previous five steps of Behavior Negotiating.

In some of the previous examples, logical consequences need not be enforced. However if Suzie continues to fight with Terry or if she continues to use inappropriate language in class, the teacher may have to change her seat or even remove her from the class. These logical consequences would be enforced only long enough to allow the teacher and Suzie to start again at step II and find a mutually agreed alternative. A similar situation would exist if Johnnie's plan to work with Caesar created a disruption for the teacher. The logical consequence would be that Johnnie would not be allowed to work with him. It may even be necessary to remove him from the class until an alternative can be found.

In Don's case the teacher must attempt to enforce a logical consequence to his disruptive behavior. She must be careful not to allow this to turn into a power struggle. The following is an example of how this might be done.

TEACHER [To Don]: *I'm sorry that you don't want to talk about this, Don. I can't allow you to be in this class if you insist on sitting on top of your desk.*

DON: *If you lay a hand on me, I'll punch you in the mouth!*

TEACHER: *You sound pretty emphatic about that.*

DON: *This school sucks. You teachers think you can push us around any time you feel like it.*

TEACHER: *You think I'm trying to push you around?*

DON: *Yeah, you and the rest of the lousy teachers here. I'm leaving.* [Don gets off his desk and walks out of class. The teacher does not try to stop him. She goes to the intercom and informs the office that Don has left. She then continues with the class.]

Behavior Negotiating did not seem to work in the situation with Don. His anger and bitterness are too deep-seated. It seems that the only option the teacher has is to continue to try to get Don to share his perceptions about school and her class. Only when she can break through—when a relationship based on an open dialogue can be established—will a meaningful change take place.

STEP VII: *Encourage and have courage.*

Rather than a sequential progression, step VII permeates the entire process of Behavior Negotiating. The importance of encouragement and courage cannot be overestimated. The two concepts may well be the foundation of all successful teaching.

Encouragement is the process of extending psychological support to the student. Inherent in this process is the teacher's belief that students' present lack of skills or inappropriate behavior in no way diminishes their value as human beings. Simply stated, *encouragement* is showing faith in students, thus enabling students to develop faith in themselves. Encouragement is given when students do not expect it, when they're not asking for it. Basic to the process is the development of trust between the teacher and student. Such trust implies that students can rely on teachers, that they can depend on a consistency and continuity in their relationship. There are hundreds of ways for teachers to show encouragement in the classroom. Unfortunately, unless the philosophy of encouragement is understood, believed, and integrated, few teachers find them.

The philosophy of encouragement is based on the belief that the teacher is able to distinguish between what a person does and what a person is. Many teachers have difficulty making this distinction. Imagine, for example, that you have done something that you consider to be stupid, thoughtless, and shortsighted. Maybe you decided to marry the town drunk, and after six months you have realized that he or she loves Scotch more than you. Or maybe you decided to quit teaching to become a gambler in Las Vegas, and you are now deeply in debt. Ponder for a moment about how you think you would feel in these or similar situations. Is there anyone with whom you would feel comfortable sharing it? Is there anyone who would listen without saying, "I told you so"? Do you know someone who would just put an arm around you and say, "It's okay." Those people understand; they try to help you work it out. If you know of such a person, then you know someone who's able to distinguish between who you are and what you do.

As teachers we often become so upset about students' cruel, thoughtless, and short-sighted behavior that we close the door on them as persons. We give up on them and are no longer willing to listen or care. While we might not say it, our actions tell these students, "I care about you only when you do what's right and good. When you don't do what's right and good, I no longer care about you." The philosophy of encouragement is based on the belief that we care—regardless. It's normal to become upset, angry, or appalled by students' behavior; valuing them in spite of their behavior is what makes it possible for them to change.

Many teachers and parents find it difficult to show unconditional caring. They might think it unimportant. They might even believe that by making their caring contingent upon acceptable behavior, they are helping the student change. Such conditional caring, however, can be devastating to children. I've worked with several lonely and insecure adolescents who were raised in such environments. One twelve-year-old girl in particular had a mother who showed love and caring only when the girl did what the mother thought was right. If the girl did something unacceptable, the mother acted cold and aloof. She would go for days without talking to the girl. Only when the daughter would finally repent and ask forgiveness would the mother again begin to care. While down deep the mother might have loved the girl regardless of her actions, her behavior did not convey this to the daughter. Consequently, the girl grew up doubting her own worth and her mother's love. She was constantly living on the edge of pain, having to measure up to her mother's expectations. During adolescence, her peer group began to provide the sense of belonging and security she needed. Finally, it became easier for her to reject her mother than to constantly try to measure up to her expectations. Unfortunately, her peer group was composed of individuals with similar insecurities. They turned to drugs and sex to try to fill the void. Today she's in a state home for delinquent girls.

Valuing human potential is the issue. To be successful at encouraging, we must believe that all individuals, regardless of how bizarre or unacceptable their behavior, have the potential to become worthwhile, contributing members of society. While the unacceptable behavior cannot be tolerated, encouraging teachers focus the bulk of their energy on developing this potential. Since the potential exists in all human beings, there's never a reason for teachers to ever give up on students. Realistically, the teacher will not always succeed. Believing that this potential exists, however, is the rationale to keep trying.

Differentiating between what a person does and what a person is, as well as believing that everyone has the potential for worthwhile behavior, enables the teacher to discover the language of encouragement. The words used are personal and unique for each teacher. They must be found within; they can't be taken from someone else's list. If we fail to integrate this belief system, then the language we use to show encouragement is phoney and artificial.

Teachers who have internalized such a belief system and who use the language of encouragement seem to have several characteristics in common:

1. *They tend to focus on students' assets rather than on their liabilities. They emphasize strengths rather than weaknesses and try to nourish and expand on these strengths. Effort and improvement are recognized and appreciated.*

2. *They try to avoid making value judgments about their students' behavior. When they like or dislike something a student does, they say so in a way that avoids judgments of goodness or badness.*

3. *They tend to respond to their students in a way that conveys acceptance. Their students don't have to be perfect to be valued.*

4. They try to show confidence and trust in their students. They believe that their students can move in positive, responsible directions. Their students eventually begin to believe this themselves.

A popular poster states, "We can complain because rose bushes have thorns, or we can rejoice because thorn bushes have roses." An encouraging teacher does the latter rather than the former.

In the example with Don, there appears to be little the teacher can do, except to keep trying. She may or may not be successful in breaking through the barrier he has built around himself. Letting him know that she cares about him as a person, that she is willing to seek him out and try again to establish a dialogue, might make the difference. She can't control how he will react, but she can decide not to give up on him.

Finally, as teachers we must have *courage*—courage to share our feelings, to confront when we must, to maintain a positive learning environment, and, most important, to keep trying in the face of adversity. It's not easy to let others know who we are and what we feel. We are often scared and even intimidated by some students. The courage needed to deal with these situations can only come by having faith and confidence in ourselves. Some of this confidence may be found in knowing that our job is to help students learn to assume the responsibility for their behavior rather than to force them into obedience.

Equally important is the courage to accept our human imperfections. We do not always confront by disclosing ourselves, nor are we always willing to listen to the student's perceptions. We find ourselves being arbitrary, angry, and aggressive. It takes courage to persist in spite of our human frailties. If we cannot, we are destined to wallow in self-pity. Because we are human we cannot be perfect.

Accepting our imperfections enables us to strive for improvement.

There are few simple solutions when working with human beings. Having confidence and courage to share our feelings and to persist when we meet failure can help.

DOES BEHAVIOR NEGOTIATING "WORK"?

The difficulty with evaluating the effectiveness of Behavior Negotiating or any other process for dealing with disruptive behavior is both philosophical, as well as methodological. What do we mean when we say, "Does it work?" Is our criterion the number of students sitting quietly in their seats doing worksheets? If this is the case, then a paddle, $50 bill, or gun often "works" quite well. Is our criterion the academic, social, and personal growth of our students? Some say that that can be accomplished without students sitting quietly in their seats doing worksheets. Suffice it to say that, as pointed out in the beginning of this chapter, Behavior Negotiating is not a technique that *solves* all your discipline problems. Rather it is a *process*, based on humanistic beliefs, for working with students whose behavior you consider to be disruptive.

The central issue is that each of us has personal criteria, based on personalities, values, and belief systems, for determining if a method "works" for us or not. If we didn't have these personal differences, we could easily learn to "solve" our discipline problems by observing the methods and techniques of teachers who have very few problems, and then teach these methods and techniques to all teachers. Unfortunately this approach does not work. The methods of the "experts" cannot be expected to work for all. Art Combs, an educational psychologist previously at the University of Florida, often talks about a study that he and others did at Syracuse when trying to help students with academic difficulties improve their study skills. Following the "emulation" line of reasoning, they assumed the best way to approach the problem was to survey the study habits of students who were doing well and then to teach these techniques to the students with difficulties. To their dismay, they discovered that the students who were doing well were frequently disorganized, studied whenever they felt like it, and often would go to a movie the night before an exam. Teaching these behaviors to students who were already failing would certainly be suicidal.

The same is true in the classroom. What works for one teacher does not necessarily work for another—especially when dealing with discipline. For example, I was told of an article offering to help teachers cut their discipline problems in half by using one amazingly simple technique, which I mentioned to a group of teachers. Although they were skeptical, they were curious to find out what the author did. I explained that she merely identified all the students who were creating discipline problems and then, very methodically, made a point to give each a big hug every day. Moans and groans filled the room. A junior high Math teacher was disappointed by such a simplistic solution. He was sure it wouldn't work for him. I indicated that I didn't know if it would or not, but I was sure of one thing: The teacher writing the article believed it worked for her.

To free us from this quagmire of a question, we must assume that since each teacher has personal criteria for determining whether an approach "works," the method for evaluating the usefulness of Behavior Negotiating must be based on teacher perception. The book's appendix reports the results of a research study designed to measure teacher perceptions of the value of Behavior Negotiating for dealing with classroom disruptions. Of the 75 teachers surveyed, over 97 percent believed that Behavior Negotiating was "highly" or "somewhat" helpful to them as an approach for dealing with disruptive behavior (Table 5 in the appendix). Further analysis revealed that teachers with a *thorough* understanding of Behavior Negotiating found the approach more "highly" helpful than teachers with a *general* or *vague* understanding of the approach (P< 0.001, Table 6). In addition, junior high teachers found the approach more "highly" helpful than did elementary teachers (P < 0.05, Table 7).

While no statistically significant differences were observed between the helpfulness of Behavior Negotiating and the proportion of minority students taught (Table 9), it is interesting to note that the only teachers who believed that Behavior Negotiating was of "no help" both taught classes composed of more than 30-percent minority students. Since the research was conducted primarily in rural schools, only 9 of the 75 teachers in the sample taught classes composed of more than 30-percent minority students. While 7 of these 9 teachers still found Behavior Negotiating "somewhat" or "highly" helpful, the effectiveness of Behavior Negotiating—and, for that matter, of other so-called "humanistic" approaches—with minority students must be raised.

BEHAVIOR NEGOTIATING AND TEACHING IN THE INNER CITY

Following the time-worn path of many other educators, I'll begin by lamenting that more research is needed to determine the effectiveness of humanistic approaches to discipline in the inner city. This is particularly true with Behavior Negotiating. Unfortunately, conducting this research is akin to pinning Jell-O on a bulletin board. The variables may be identified, but they seem to defy quantifying. Nevertheless, without data to verify or refute humanistic approaches in ghetto schools, we continue to consciously or unconsciously dichotomize our approaches. We use warmth and understanding with the nice, clean, polite middle-class kids who agree with our goals and values. Yet we tend to use fear, threats, and power with the Blacks, Puerto Ricans, Chicanos, and poor whites who disagree. The data in the appendix indicates that teachers believe Behavior Negotiating "works" quite well in the first case. Further research is needed in the latter.

The issue is broader than just the effectiveness of Behavior Negotiating in the inner city. We must deal with the entire concept of humanism in environments where the goals and values of the students seem diametrically opposed to those of the teacher. In environments where students have been brought up valuing physical retaliation, warmth and understanding are often seen as weaknesses. So called "humanistic" teachers are laughed at, ridiculed, and pushed around. They are forced to either come out swinging or sell insurance. Herb Foster, in his book, *Ribbin', Jivin' and Playin' the Dozens*, has documented many examples of these conflicts.[6] In addition, his "Four-Phase Rites of Passage" describes the process that most inner-city secondary teachers learn to deal with discipline. I've observed similar phases in many suburban teachers, as well. I include them here to emphasize that there is no contradiction between Behavior Negotiating and firmness.

The first phase can be called *permissivism*. Similar to Foster's "friends" phase, beginning teachers face the classroom filled with insecurity. Uncertain about their relationship with the students and wanting to avoid the role of "dictator," they approach the class with a warm, friendly disposition, hoping that by treating the students as "adults" they will respond in mature ways. As Foster says, "He entered his new job with idealism, warmheartedly, and full of hope; he really wants to do a good job. He wants to like his students and he wants his students to like him."[7] This is a difficult and trying time for new teachers. Their insecurities and uncertainties cause them to personalize everything students say and do. Desperately needing to feel successful and liked, they believe that understanding and caring are the keys to this success. While I believe that they are right, the realities of American classrooms come as a shock. Foster's description of his first day in a ghetto school can't help but start the knees shaking on anyone who must face such an environment:

After lunch, about 10 to 15 minutes into the first of three periods, I noticed a youngster run out of the back door of my classroom. When I closed the back door, another youngster ran out of the front door of my classroom also leaving it open. After briefly watching some of my students run in and out of the front and back doors, I realized that they were the same ones who were going in and out of the doors. They were not running out and leaving . . .

Next, I discovered a new word–"Teach". One of the youngsters walked up to me and said, "Hey, Teach, we work a period, read comics a period, and then take off the last period—OK?" To which I responded with something like, "Look, I'm a vet and I'm the teacher now. I intend to stay, and we are going to work all three periods."

From then on everything seemed to happen at once. Someone crumpled up a piece of paper and threw it at me with a near miss. I thought of my Psychology I and II courses ("make a joke out of things"—or—"Decontaminate through humor") so I said, "If that's the best you can do you better hang it up." Whereupon all hell broke loose. The class was going to show me they could do better!

Students ran across the table tops throwing T-squares and drawing boards. Others ran in and out of the room. The noise was deafening. T-square and drawing board missiles flew through the air. The classroom was not only noisy but dangerous. And you know what I did? You know that section that is

cut out of the teacher's desk where the teacher puts his legs when
he sits down? I hid there—in the kneehole.

Suddenly, five or six teachers stuck their heads into the room to
see what was going on. I looked up sheepishly from my shelter
without saying a word. Since the din continued even with their
presence, they threw both doors open and my students took off.[8]

The second phase can be called *disillusionment*. According to
Foster it's a period of rejection and chaos. Teachers, questioning
their belief system, experience frustration and isolation. The students are pushing and testing while teachers doubt their original
belief that caring and warmth are important. Some honest soul-
searching may take place, or the teacher may simply "blame" the
students and/or the system for being so primitive and unresponsive.
The choices are either move to phase three, find an "easier" school,
or leave the profession.

Foster calls phase three *discipline*. I prefer the term *control*. This
is when the teacher begins to establish order out of the chaos.
Firmness and toughness become essential. The teacher is no longer
willing to tolerate the games the students are playing. As Foster says,
"At this phase, some sensitive teachers begin to hate themselves for
what they are doing in the name of discipline. (I tell new teachers
when they begin to hate themselves for this toughness, they are
beginning to grow and make it as teachers . .)."[9]

I believe that many teachers reject Behavior Negotiating and
other humanistic approaches during this phase. A sense of smug
cynicism sets in. "I've tried that humanistic crap, and it just doesn't
work with these kids" is a statement I've heard from many teachers.
Bitterness and resentment are common among teachers at this
phase. They feel betrayed and are no longer willing to trust
"humanistic types." They have equated humanism with first-phase

permissivism and, after a painful period of disillusionment, have rejected both. They are resigned to the toughness of the third phase.

A small number of teachers eventually move beyond phase 3 to phase 4: *humanism*. Again, Foster's description is valuable, "The phase 4 classroom has a relaxed atmosphere where feelings are expressed. The students have run their testing games and have learned their teacher's limits. Learning takes place in this positive, structured, yet relaxed atmosphere. Students move around the room knowing that no one will pick on them, that no one will steal their clothing from the closet, and that their teacher is fair and will answer their questions. He respects them and they respect him. Their teacher is in charge and in control; and they can now relax."[10]

The transition from phase 3 to phase 4 is not smooth and easy. Few teachers make it. Foster estimates that between 70 and 80 percent of the teachers in ghetto schools are fixated at phase 3. Distrustful of students, they are continuously on guard, maintaining control through fear and busywork. In order to make this transition, it is crucial that teachers be able to differentiate between humanism and permissivism. To be humanistic does not mean to abdicate our control of the classroom.

Humanistic methods for dealing with discipline problems can and do work in inner-city schools. Yes, we need control—learning cannot take place in chaos. Establishing this control, however, does not mean we have to disregard caring and understanding, even though some students may perceive it as weakness. Behavior Negotiating is based on caring, understanding, and firmness. This firmness is not derived from totalitarianism and personal power needs; it is rather based on maintaining order and control by negotiating conflicts and enforcing logical consequences when necessary. Our goal is to create and maintain a social order that allows all students an opportunity to grow and learn without fear.

BEHAVIOR NEGOTIATING BY PARENTS

Although most of the previous examples used to describe Behavior Negotiating demonstrate conflicts between teachers and students, the approach is also useful for resolving conflicts between parents and their children. Successful negotiation of these conflicts, however, depends on the nature and quality of the parent–child relationship that has developed since birth.

No one asks to be born. We are brought into this world by forces beyond our control. From the warmth and security of the womb, we are suddenly catapulted into a strange and frightening environment. Our choices are limited—adapt or die. Even without the doctor's slap there is good reason to cry. From this abrupt beginning, all infants must learn to satisfy their needs. Most learn quickly. They discover that by acting totally obnoxious, they make adults attend to them. It's a fact of life: Screaming babies get fed and diapered.

Fortunately for parents, babies grow up. As they do, we try to teach them to satisfy their needs through socially acceptable alternatives to screaming and crying. Rather than yelling and kicking, the child is now taught to make polite, courteous requests. This period of retraining is often difficult for both parties. Parents must learn to be firm and consistent, and children must learn to delay gratification. "Terrible-twos" and "trying threes" are terms often used to describe the beginning stages of this retraining. Many parents have difficulty finding the firmness necessary to weather this period.

I observed such a situation during one of my weekly grocery shopping trips (since my "consciousness" has been raised, I do half the cooking and all the grocery shopping in our family). A young mother happened to be shopping with a two- or three-year-old boy hanging from her basket. Following them some distance back, I noticed that she was making a crucial error by stopping in the candy aisle to talk to another shopper. (Shopping with my five-year-old son, I have learned to triple my speed through this area.) As she was standing there talking, little junior suddenly recognized the delights that surrounded him and began pointing and shouting, "Candy, candy," with a big smile of anticipation on his face. As I passed, I heard her say loudly and firmly, "No, no, Billy." She then returned to her conversation with her friend. Well, Billy was not about to end the matter here. He began to shout as loudly as he could, "Candy, candy, I want candy," and then began a siren-like scream that resonated throughout the store. The mother escalated her "no, no" commands, but these merely served to oil the little siren that was now causing all in the store to stop and take notice. The battle raged on for an embarrassing length of time, causing even the stoic-looking meatcutter to wince. Finally, the screaming ended as abruptly as it had started. As I again passed the candy aisle on my way to the checkout counter, I noticed Billy's mother still in conversation with her friend. As I politely smiled, Billy grinned up at me from his mother's cart with the wet chocolate from a king-size Tootsie Roll running down the sides of his mouth.

You don't need a degree in child psychology to understand what Billy learned from this encounter. I just hope I'm not in the store the next time his mother decides *not* to give him some candy. While not all the steps of Behavior Negotiating are appropriate with a two- or three-year-old, most are still applicable—even at this age. In a conflict like the one experienced by Billy's mother, the last step, having courage, seems to be the most important. Many situations force us as parents to say "no" to our children. When we do, we need the courage to *mean it*. If children learn that "no" means, "yes, if I scream loud enough," then we are on the road to making our lives and our children's lives miserable. This is not an easy task. It requires a great deal of courage and confidence to be firm and consistent. Scolding, moralizing, and preaching are relatively useless. When we say "no," we must mean it. Consequently, the decision to say "no" must be based on a full awareness of what actions may be necessary to enforce it.

Before making this decision, it is often useful to decide which factors or contingencies in a conflict are negotiable. In the example with Billy and his mother, we have a little boy who sees candy and decides he wants some—a normal reaction. Billy's mother decides either to buy it or not, based on her "rules" for the situation. She may have a clear-cut policy of never buying candy when she is grocery shopping or never buying it before dinner. More likely, she doesn't have a firm policy. She makes the decision each week based on her mood, budget, or Billy's previous intake of snacks. For some reason, on this particular day, she decides not to buy it. To this point there really is no problem for the mother. Billy, however, views the situation differently. He wants the candy now, and he is not willing either to wait until after dinner or to agree that he has had too much already. I believe that when his mother denies the request, it is important for her to calmly and simply explain her reason, even though Billy may not understand or accept it. There is no value in arguing or in trying to persuade Billy that she is acting in his best interest. Rarely will a two-year-old say, "You're right, mother. It probably will spoil my dinner. Thank you for not buying it." Only when Billy starts his screaming and shouting does the mother begin to experience a problem. Step I, disclosing her feelings, is now appropriate. This disclosure is not likely to change Billy's behavior, but it will maintain an honesty in the dialogue. Something like, "Billy, when you scream and shout, I get a headache" or "Billy, your crying is upsetting me" is all that is necessary. There's no reason to repeat it—once is enough. In this case, Billy will likely ignore his mother and continue his tantrum.

Step II, encouraging him to share his perception of the situation, is probably not necessary. He sees candy, wants it, and is angry and upset because mother won't give it to him. She might want to acknowledge her understanding of this by saying, "I know it's hard for you to see the candy and not be able to have it, Billy." Some parents may believe that if Billy is screaming and shouting, he's not going to hear this. If he does, he probably does not understand or accept it. For these reasons, they believe it more beneficial to wait until the tantrum is finished before acknowledging his feelings. There is value in both approaches. When we wait until he has calmed down, he is more likely to hear us and realize we do understand his feelings. On the other hand, by acknowledging his feelings during the conflict, we keep a clear picture of what's happening with Billy and what's happening with ourselves. The clearer our understanding of these feelings, the more effective we will be in resolving the conflict.

In either case, little more need be said. We must now *act*. Moralizing, threatening and cajoling serve no purpose. Having the child examine his motives or explore alternatives are relatively useless during a temper tantrum. Natural or logical consequences must be imposed. In this case, the natural consequence is to allow Billy to continue his screaming and crying until he tires of it and stops. This takes strength and courage on the part of mother, especially in front of the jaundiced eye of the meatcutter. Nevertheless, firmly ignoring such outbursts is one of the most effective ways to extinguish them. Be warned, however, when you ignore temper tantrums or bids for attention, they will get *worse* before they get better. An alternative, logical action is to remove Billy from the store and let him cry outside. If he fights, kicks, or starts running, you may have to carry him calmly to the car. I believe it is important to avoid yelling, scolding, or even raising your voice when you do this. Billy eventually discovers that the tantrum does not manipulate his mother into giving him his way. How long this takes is directly related to the number of times she has given into him in the past. Only when he has calmed down should she again discuss the issue.

Behavior Negotiating is most effective when children examine their motives and evaluate the consequences of their behavior. It is difficult to determine at what age a child is capable of achieving this task. I have found that many four-, five-, and six-year-olds can verbally evaluate their behavior and discuss its effect on themselves and others. Infants and younger children can understand the relationship between their behavior and consequences, but often are not able to verbalize it. Step V, making a commitment to alternative behavior is successful only after such an understanding takes place. We cannot *demand* that Billy stop his tantrum, we can only help him discover that such behavior does not meet his needs.

Negotiating conflicts with older children and adolescents is much more complicated. Our success is often related to the history of prior conflicts we have experienced with the child. After having been a dictator or doormat for ten or twelve years, we can't expect to suddenly change behavior with Behavior Negotiating. Furthermore, conflicts between parents and older children often center around value-laden issues: the length of hair, smoking, curfew times, and dating rather than with overt disruptions. With this in mind, the following suggestions are offered to parents of older children for helping them increase their effectiveness with Behavior Negotiating.

Many conflicts can be avoided by negotiating the limits of acceptable and unacceptable behavior before problems arise.

If parents and their children can agree on their rules and procedures ahead of time, transgressions are much easier to resolve. This is particularly true when dealing with value issues.

I recently experienced a conflict with my ten-year-old daughter concerning her TV viewing habits, which relates to this point. I was feeling annoyed and disappointed at her spending too much time watching prime-time garbage. When I confronted her with these feelings, she became defensive. It was my opinion that weekly stories about bikini-clad blondes and gun-shooting macho gangsters were unrealistic and somewhat inappropriate for a ten-year-old. Her opinion differed. She believed them to be entertaining and exciting, and besides, *everyone* in her fifth-grade class thinks they're "neat." Not wanting to singlehandedly attack the opinions and values of her entire fifth grade, I countered with the importance of homework and recreational reading. Since she has always done well in school and is a voracious reader to boot, I was losing ground. Her values and mine differed over this issue, and we were unable to negotiate step IV of Behavior Negotiating.

At this point, I could have used force to change her behavior by taking away her allowance, by tripping the circuit breaker on the TV outlet, or by demanding that she go to her room. Such actions, of course, would have produced considerable resentment and anger on her part. Instead, I decided to skirt the value issue of what constitutes a good or bad program and to focus on negotiating some rules for TV viewing. She agreed to discuss the matter and then offered to limit her viewing time to three hours a day. Believing that anything more than a half-hour was too much, I shuddered. After some give and take on both sides, we eventually agreed that she would limit herself to a maximum of one hour of prime-time viewing. She would have freedom to watch whatever she wanted, and I was barred from sitting in back of the room and heckling the actors or making fun of the plot (a habit I had acquired while watching some of the prime-time shows). We also agreed that any additional viewing would require *my* prior approval. Since clarifying our rules, we have ended our conflict over this issue. Although I secretly wish she would completely avoid the weekly prime-time serials, I have noticed that she is becoming more selective in spending her precious hour.

As mentioned above, we need the courage to enforce decisions that we believe are in the child's best interest.

Some parents believe that older children necessitate the use of power to enforce these decisions. I disagree. As children grow older, we must rely more and more on the use of logical consequences rather than personal power to enforce decisions. Each time we use force to overpower a child, we chip away at the trust and responsibility so important to good parent–child relationships. Furthermore, the more we rely on power to resolve conflicts, the more bitterness and resentment we produce in the child. Children, being continually overpowered, develop a feeling of powerlessness that causes them to strike out in attempts to establish their own sense of power.

Consequently, as children get older we must make every possible effort to negotiate a mutually agreed solution to the conflicts we encounter. Logical consequences occasionally need to be enforced, but there are differences between enforcing logical consequences and using force to overpower and punish a child. These differences have been discussed earlier in this chapter, and they become more significant as the child grows older. When enforcing a logical consequence, the child might still respond with resentment and anger. It is important therefore to always try to reestablish the trust that may have been damaged. Discussing the relationship between the child's behavior and the logical consequence *after* the anger and resentment have dissipated and constantly striving to negotiate future conflicts are two ways to preserve trust.

As parents, we should try to show our children at least the same respect we show the Avon Lady.

I have written much about respect in this book. Here I want to focus on the words and tone of voice we use when talking with our children. When the Avon Lady, any friend, or a neighbor for that matter spills a cup of coffee or a drink on our living room carpet, take note at how we generally react and the tone of voice we use. The adult is usually embarrassed and apologetic. We quickly get a damp cloth, wipe the spill, and try to soothe the culprit by saying something like, "Oh, don't worry about it. It needed cleaning anyway," or "Those coffee mugs sure are wobbly. I should have given you a coaster for it." Now observe what happens when our son or daughter spills a glass of milk on the same carpet. Are we just as calm and polite? Is our tone of voice soothing and reassuring? Probably not. Many parents see this as an opportunity to critically assess the child's manual dexterity ("I swear, you're the clumsiest child I have ever seen!"), to become a practicing historian ("You did the same damn thing last month!"), and to ponder philosophical perplexities ("How could you be so inconsiderate. I just cleaned yesterday!"). All the while, we assume that the child has developed a sudden ear affliction that necessitates shouting as loudly as possible.

Why are we more considerate of the Avon Lady than we are of our own children? Maybe it's because we believe the Avon Lady wouldn't understand our emotional outburst and would think badly of us. Or maybe because yelling criticisms, threats, and commands at our children provides a cathartic release. Some may even believe that these outbursts are part of their obligation to *teach* their child acceptable ways of behaving. More often, however, they produce resentment, defensiveness, sever the threads of open communication, and cause the child to internalize a failure identity. Fortunately, kids are wonderfully resilient, and we need not always protect them from our feelings and emotions. If we can try to avoid name-calling and labeling, and if we can maintain an equal balance between the number of times we yell and scold and the number of times we show love, warmth, and encouragement, then children can still believe they are lovable and capable. The devastation comes when we fall into habitual patterns of yelling, scolding, and criticizing.

The effectiveness of negotiating conflicts with an older child is increased if the child has internalized a feeling of being lovable and capable.

This feeling does not develop automatically. It must be nurtured by parents through the process of encouragement. Previously discussed in this chapter, the process of encouragement is probably the single most important skill in child rearing. Most parents possess the skill, and they are quite effective in using it with younger children. Unfortunately, as the child grows older they often forget its importance.

Evidence that parents are skillful in the process of encouragement is readily demonstrated when we observe parents teaching their young child to walk. Although few of us can remember the experience, learning to walk was a difficult task requiring much trial and error and an ability to overcome failure. Nevertheless, most parents demonstrate an exceptionally effective ability to show encouargement during this difficult time. When wobbly little Billy begins cautiously to take that inevitable first step, mother or father is there with a big smile of anticipation and warm words of support. When he tumbles over on his behind, one of the parents is there to pick him up and soothe the hurt. Rarely does mother say, "Billy, that's the fifth time you've fallen this morning. Now get up and do it right!" If father was at work during this exciting time, mother anxiously awaits his arrival to tell of Billy's success. As he opens the door she happily shouts, "Guess what? Billy took two steps today!" Father breaks out with a big smile and runs to give the little tyke a hug. Rarely does mother say to father, "Guess what? Billy was trying to walk today and fell twelve times!" It is also unlikely that father says, "Billy, you really should try to stop falling so much, it's hard on the furniture." No, when we teach our children to walk, we focus on success rather than failure. We provide faith and support for the child, and we show excitement and approval with each improvement. We know *how* to encourage—remembering to do it during all the stages of our children's development is what's often overlooked.

Finally, we need to forgive our human imperfections.

Not a parent alive *always* says or does the right thing at the right time. Because we are human, we make mistakes. We yell when we know we should listen, and we are arbitrary when we know we should negotiate. Our pent-up emotions are often vented on our children. The myriad of problems experienced with day-to-day living with other human beings make it impossible to do otherwise. Accepting these shortcomings enables us to forgive ourselves and to repair any damages we have caused. We cannot demand perfection in our children, nor can we expect it in ourselves.

There are no panaceas or shortcut solutions when it comes to finding ways to resolve conflicts with kids. Kim Hubbard's classic comment about success in life is equally applicable to success with kids, "The secret to success is this. There is no secret to success." Having the courage to believe in ourselves, to be open and honest with our feelings, and to show faith and trust in our children—all these things enable us to make an honest search.

The following research study was designed to measure teachers' perceptions of their understanding of Behavior Negotiating and their opinions of its usefulness with helping them deal with disruptive behavior in their classrooms.

The 75 teachers who enrolled in two sections of the course, "Understanding and Dealing with Disruptive Classroom Behavior," comprise the population for the study. One section was taught by the author, and the other was team-taught by the author and a colleague. The course included an overview of both tension-reduction and need-satisfaction disruptive behavior. Emphasis was placed on finding ways to prevent as well as to deal with classroom disruptions. Training in Glasser's Reality Therapy, Gordon's Conflict Resolution, Dreikur's Democratic Methods, and Behavior Negotiating was provided. The classes met once for two and a half hours each week, and approximately six weeks were devoted exclu-

APPENDIX:

(research on behavior negotiating)

sively to Behavior Negotiating. At the completion of the course an anonymous questionnaire was administered to each teacher. In addition to demographic data, teachers were asked to rate their personal understanding of Behavior Negotiating and their opinion of the helpfulness of Behavior Negotiating for dealing with classroom discipline problems. Tables 1, 2, and 3 report the number and percentage of teachers teaching at various grade levels, their years of teaching experience, and the proportion of minority students taught for the 75 teachers enrolled in the course.

1: GRADE LEVEL TAUGHT

GRADE LEVEL	NUMBER OF TEACHERS	PERCENTAGE
Elementary	45	60.0
Junior high	10	13.3
High school	20	26.7
TOTAL	75	100.0

2: YEARS OF TEACHING EXPERIENCE

YEARS OF EXPERIENCE	NUMBER OF TEACHERS	PERCENTAGE
1–3 years	13	17.3
3–6 years	24	32.0
6–10 years	20	26.7
Over 10 years	18	24.0
TOTAL	75	100.0

PROPORTION OF MINORITY STUDENTS	NUMBER OF TEACHERS	PERCENTAGE
Less than 10%	47	62.7
10–30%	19	26.3
Over 30%	9	12.0
TOTAL	75	100.0

Table 4 reports the teachers' perceptions of their understanding of Behavior Negotiating.

4: Understanding of Behavior Negotiating

UNDERSTANDING	NUMBER OF TEACHERS	PERCENTAGE
Thorough understanding	20	26.7
General understanding	50	66.7
Vague understanding	5	6.6
TOTAL	75	100.0

Table 5 reports teachers' opinions of the helpfulness of Behavior Negotiating for dealing with their discipline problems.

5: Helpfulness of Behavior Negotiating for Dealing With Problems

HELPFULNESS	NUMBER OF TEACHERS	PERCENTAGE
Highly helpful	41	54.7
Somewhat helpful	32	42.7
No help	2	2.6
TOTAL	75	100.0

The Chi Square statistic was used to determine whether significant differences in teacher perception of the helpfulness of Behavior Negotiating was related to (1) teacher understanding of Behavior Negotiating, (2) the grade level taught, (3) years of teaching experience, or (4) the proportion of minority students taught. The Null Hypothesis was assumed. Tables 6 through 9 report the results of these comparisons.

6: HELPFULNESS OF BEHAVIOR NEGOTIATING AS
A FUNCTION OF TEACHER UUNDERSTANDING

UNDERSTANDING	HIGHLY HELPFUL	SOMEWHAT HELPFUL	NO HELP	TOTAL
Thorough understanding	29	2	0	31
General understanding	11	25	2	38
Vague understanding	1	5	0	6
TOTAL	41	32	2	75

Small expected cell frequencies required the collapsing of the "Somewhat Helpful" and "No Help" columns, as well as the "General" and "Vague" understanding rows.

The results show that the helpfulness of Behavior Negotiating is significantly related to the understanding of Behavior Negotiating ($X^2 = 28.3$, $P < 0.001$, $df = 1$). Teachers with a thorough understanding of Behavior Negotiating found it more highly helpful for dealing with their disruptive behavior than teachers with a general or vague understanding of the approach.

7: HELPFULNESS OF BEHAVIOR NEGOTIATING AS RELATED TO GRADE LEVEL TAUGHT

GRADE LEVEL	HIGHLY HELPFUL	SOMEWHAT HELPFUL	NO HELP	TOTAL
Elementary	20	23	2	45
Junior high	9	1	0	10
High school	11	9	0	20
TOTAL	41	32	2	75

Small expected cell frequencies required the collapsing of the "Somewhat Helpful" and "No Help" columns for analysis with Chi Square. Significant differences in the helpfulness of Behavior Negotiating occur as a function of grade level taught ($X^2 = 7.06$, $P < 0.05$). Further analysis revealed that junior high school teachers found Behavior Negotiating more helpful for dealing with class disruption than did elementary teachers.

8: HELPFULNESS OF BEHAVIOR NEGOTIATING AS RELATED TO TEACHING EXPERIENCE

EXPERIENCE	HIGHLY HELPFUL	SOMEWHAT HELPFUL	NO HELP	TOTAL
1–3 years	10	3	0	13
3–6 years	13	10	1	24
6–10 years	10	10	0	20
Over 10 years	8	8	$	17
TOTAL	41	31	2	74

Small expected cell frequencies required the collapsing of the "Somewhat Helpful" and "No Help" columns. No significant differences in the helpfulness of Behavior Negotiating occur as a function of teaching experience ($X^2 = 3.22$, $P > 0.05$).

9: HELPFULNESS OF BEHAVIOR NEGOTIATING
AS RELATED TO PROPORTION OF MINORITY STUDENTS TAUGHT

PROPORTION OF MINORITY STUDENTS	HIGHLY HELPFUL	SOMEWHAT HELPFUL	NO HELP	TOTAL
Less than 10%	25	22	0	47
10–30%	12	7	0	19
Over 30%	4	3	2	9
TOTAL	41	32	2	75

Again, small expected cell frequencies required the collapsing of the "Somewhat Helpful" and "No Help" columns. The results indicate that no statistically significant differences were observed in the helpfulness of Behavior Negotiating as related to the proportion of minority students taught ($X^2 = 1.13$, $P > 0.05$).

BENJAMIN, ALFRED, *The Helping Interview* (2nd ed.). Boston: Houghton Mifflin Co., 1974. Provides training in listening skills, and emphasizes the importance of acceptance and empathy when helping others.

BROWN, GEORGE, *Human Teaching for Human Learning*. New York: The Viking Press, 1971. Integrates the cognitive and affective domains of the classroom into what Brown has termed "confluent education."

BUSCAGLIA, LEO, *Love*. Thorofare, N.J.: Charles Slack, Inc., 1972. Essential reading for understanding ourselves and our relationships with others.

BUSHELL, DON, *Classroom Behavior: A Little Book for Teachers*. Englewood Cliffs, N.J.: Prentice-Hall, Inc., 1973.

SELECTED BIBLIOGRAPHY

CARTER, RONALD, *Help! These Kids are Driving Me Crazy*. Champaign, Ill.: Research Press, Inc., 1972. Provides a behavior modification approach to discipline.

CLARIZIO, HARVEY, *Toward Positive Classroom Discipline*. New York: John Wiley & Sons, Inc., 1971. Provides a behavior modification approach to discipline.

CULLUM, ALBERT, *The Geranium on the Window Sill Just Died, but Teacher You Went Right On*. Holland: Harlin Quist, Inc., 1971. A powerful collection of poems and illustrations that reflect the perceptions children have of their teachers.

DINKMEYER, DON AND RUDOLF DREIKURS, *Encouraging Children to Learn: The Encouragement Process*. Englewood Cliffs, N.J.: Prentice-Hall, Inc., 1963. A classic description of what it means to encourage others.

DINKMEYER, DON AND GARY MCKAY, *Systematic Training for Effective Parenting, Parent's Handbook*. Circle Pines, Minn.: American Guidance Services, Inc., 1976.

DOBSON, JAMES, *Dare to Discipline*. Glendale, Cal.: Regal Books, 1972. His advice to parents of young children is of particular value.

DOLLAR, BERRY, *Humanizing Classroom Discipline: A Behavioral Approach*. New York: Harper & Row, Publishers, Inc., 1972. An attempt to integrate the behavioral and humanistic approaches to discipline.

DREIKURS, RUDOLF AND VICKI SOLTZ, *Children: The Challenge*. New York: Hawthorn Books, Inc., 1964. An excellent book for parents that gives a complete description of democratic child raising.

———, *Psychology in the Classroom: A Manual for Teachers* (2nd ed.). New York: Harper & Row, Publishers, Inc., 1968.

————, Bernice Bronia Grunwald, and Floy Pepper, *Maintaining Sanity in the Classroom: Illustrated Teaching Techniques*. New York: Harper & Row, Publishers, Inc., 1971. Provides a complete account of the motives of disruptive students, and discusses democratic ways for dealing with them.

———— and Pearl Cassel, *Discipline Without Tears*. New York: Hawthorn Books, Inc., 1974.

Epstein, Charlotte, *Classroom Management and Teaching: Persistent Problems and Rational Solutions*. Reston, Va.: Reston Publishing Co., 1979.

Foster, Herbert, *Ribbin', Jivin', and Playin' the Dozens*. Cambridge, Mass.: Ballinger Publishing Co., 1974. An excellent book for helping teachers understand the games of inner-city students.

Gazda, George et. al., *Human Relations Development: A Manual for Educators* (2nd ed.). Boston: Allyn & Bacon, Inc., 1977. Provides systematic training for improving listening and helping skills.

Ginott, Haim, *Teacher and Child*. New York: Macmillan, Inc., 1972. A book filled with anecdotes and scenarios designed to help teachers relate more effectively to students.

Glasser, William, *Reality Therapy*. New York: Harper & Row, Publishers, Inc., 1965.

————, *Schools Without Failure*. New York: Harper & Row, Publishers, Inc., 1969. Provides the basics of Glasser's educational philosophy.

————, *The Effects of School Failure on the Life of a Child.*

Washington, D.C.: National Association of Elementary School Principals, 1971.

―――, *The Identity Society*. New York: Harper & Row, Publishers, Inc., 1972. Describes a changing generation of youth that lends support to a "generation gap" view of schools.

GORDON, THOMAS, *Parent Effectiveness Training*. New York: P. H. Wyden, 1970.

―――, *Teacher Effectiveness Training*. New York: P. H. Wyden, 1974. Provides a detailed description of active listening, I-messages, and conflict resolution in the classroom.

GREENBERG, HERBERT, *Teaching With Feeling*. Indianapolis: The Bobbs-Merrill Co., Inc. (Pegasus), 1969. Provides insight to the many frustrations experienced by teachers.

GRUHLKE, VERNA, *To Hell With the Kids*. Riverside, N.J.: Macmillan, Inc., (Bruce Books), 1968.

HOLT, JOHN, *How Children Fail*. New York: Pitman Publishing Co., 1964. A classic for understanding both children and school failure.

HOUSE, ERNEST AND STEVE LAPAN, *Survival in the Classroom*. Boston: Allyn and Bacon, Inc., 1978.

JESSUP, MICHAEL AND MARGARET KILEY, *Discipline: Positive Attitudes for Learning*. Englewood Cliffs, N.J.: Prentice-Hall, Inc., 1971.

JONES, ALAN, *Students, Don't Push Your Teacher Down the Stairs on Friday*. New York: Quadrangle Books, 1972.

KARLIN, MURIAL AND REGINA BERGER, *Discipline and the Disruptive Child: A Practical Guide for Elementary School Teachers*. Englewood Cliffs, N.J.: Prentice-Hall, Inc., 1972.

KOUNIN, JACOB, *Discipline and Group Management in Classrooms*. New York: Holt, Rinehart and Winston, 1970.

KRUMBOLTZ, JOHN AND HELEN KRUMBOLTZ, *Changing Children's Behavior*. Englewood Cliffs, N.J.: Prentice-Hall, Inc., 1972. Provides a behavior modification view of discipline. Filled with many examples.

LAGRAND, LOUIS, *Discipline in the Secondary School*. Englewood Cliffs, N.J.: Prentice-Hall, Inc., 1969.

LARSON, KNUTE, *School Discipline in an Age of Rebellion*. West Nyack, N.Y.: Parker Publishing Co., 1972.

LONG, NICHOLAS, WILLIAM MORSE, AND RUTH NEWMAN, eds., *Conflict in the Classroom: The Education of Children With Problems* (2nd ed.). Belmont, Cal.: Wadsworth Publishing Co., 1971. An outstanding collection of articles for understanding and dealing with children with emotional problems.

MADSON, CHARLES AND CLIFFORD MADSON, *Teaching Discipline: A Positive Approach for Educational Development* (2nd ed.). Boston: Allyn and Bacon, Inc., 1974.

MILGRAM, STANLEY, *Obedience to Authority: An Experimental View*. New York: Harper & Row, Publishers, Inc., 1974. Presents the complete design and results of Milgram's obedience research.

MOUSTAKES, CLARK, *Who Will Listen?* New York: Ballantine Books, Inc., 1975.

RYAN, KEVIN, ed., *Don't Smile Until Christmas; Accounts of the First Year of Teaching*. Chicago: University of Chicago Press, 1970.

WALLEN, CARL AND LADONNA WALLEN, *Effective Classroom Man-*

agement. Boston: Allyn and Bacon, Inc., 1978. Provides a "management" view of teaching and dealing with discipline.

WEES, WILFORD, *Nobody Can Teach Anyone Anything.* New York: Doubleday & Co., Inc., 1971.

WIENER, DANIEL, *Classroom Management and Discipline.* Itasca, Ill.: F. E. Peacock Publishers, Inc., 1972. Presents many problem situations with trial solutions.

CHAPTER 1

[1]Stanley Milgram, *Obedience to Authority: An Experimental View* (New York: Harper & Row, 1974).

[2]Milgram, *Obedience to Authority*, p. 21.

[3]Don Hamachek, "Removing the Stigma from Obedience Behavior," *Phi Delta Kappan*, 57, No. 7 (March 1976), 443–47.

[4]William Glasser, *The Identity Society* (New York: Harper & Row, 1972).

[5]Glasser, *The Identity Society*, pp. 27–54.

CHAPTER NOTES

CHAPTER 2

[1]Dean Lobaugh, "Why Do We Have to Study This?" *Nation's Schools*, 51, No. 4 (April 1953), 51–52. Copyright © 1953, McGraw–Hill, Inc.

[2]Rudolf Dreikurs, *Psychology in the Classroom* (New York: Harper & Row, 1957), pp. 12–17.

[3]Don Dinkmeyer and Jon Carlson, "Consequences—Cues to Understanding Behavior," *Elementary School Journal* (April 1973), pp. 399–404.

[4]Revised from Jon Carlson and Brenda Rifkin Farber, "Necessary Skills for Parenting," *Focus on Guidance*, 8, No. 7, March 1976 (Denver: Love Publishing Co.), p. 3.

CHAPTER 3

[1]William Glasser, *The Effects of School Failure on the Life of a Child* (Washington, D.C.: National Association of Elementary School Principals, 1971).

[2]Robert Rosenthal and Lenore Jacobson, *Pygmalion in the Classroom* (New York: Holt, Rinehart and Winston, Inc., 1968).

[3]George Mouly, *Psychology for Effective Teaching*, 2nd ed. (New York: Holt, Rinehart and Winston, Inc., 1968), p. 89.

CHAPTER 4

[1]Thomas Gordon, *Teacher Effectiveness Training* (New York: P. H. Wyden, 1974), pp. 19–43.

[2]Revised from George Gazda et al, *Human Relations Development: A Manual for Educators*, 2nd ed. (Boston: Allyn and Bacon, Inc., 1977), pp. 47–50.

[3]Gordon, *Teacher Effectiveness Training*, pp. 142–45.

[4]Revised from F. Gilbert (n.p.) as quoted by Ruth Harris, "How to Deal With the Pain of Rejection," *Cosmopolitan*, 181, No. 2 (August 1976), p. 149.

[5]Gazda, *Human Relations Development*, pp. 19–24.

[6]Revised from Gazda, *Human Relations Development*, pp. 47–50.

CHAPTER 5
[1]William Glasser, *Reality Therapy* (New York: Harper & Row, 1965).

[2]Thomas Gordon, *Teacher Effectiveness Training* (New York: P. H. Wyden, 1974), pp. 19–43.

[3]Gordon, *Teacher Effectiveness Training*, pp. 227–34.

[4]Rudolf Dreikurs, *Psychology in the Classroom*, 2nd ed. (New York: Harper & Row, 1968) and Rudolf Dreikurs, Bernice Bronia Grunwald, and Floy Pepper, *Maintaining Sanity in the Classroom: Illustrated Teaching Techniques* (New York: Harper & Row, 1971).

[5]Rudolf Dreikurs and Pearl Cassel, *Discipline Without Tears*, 2nd ed. (New York: Hawthorn Books, Inc., 1974), p. 44.

[6]Herbert Foster, *Ribbin', Jivin', and Playin' the Dozens* (Cambridge, Mass.: Ballinger Publishing Co., 1974).

[7]Foster, *Ribbin'*, p. 239.

[8]Foster, *Ribbin'*, p. 8.

[9]Foster, *Ribbin'*, p. 243.

[10]Foster, *Ribbin'*, p. 243.

INDEX